PRAISE FOR *BIRDS OF PRAY*

If you're a football fan you likely know the story of the 2017 Philadelphia Eagles on the field. Winning the Super Bowl was a tremendous accomplishment, but it is only half the story. *Birds of Pray* will give you a look at what really made the Eagles special—the tremendous spiritual bond they developed through Jesus Christ.

> TONY DUNGY, Head Coach of Super Bowl XLI
> champion Indianapolis Colts

In *Birds of Pray*, Rob Maaddi captures the story of our brotherhood and the special bond we have in Christ that helped us become Super Bowl champions.

> CARSON WENTZ, Philadelphia Eagles Pro Bowl
> quarterback

We wanted to win the Super Bowl. But we also knew making disciples of Jesus is our number one priority. Rob was there to see and hear that. From the pre-game huddles to baptisms in the cold tub and all the moments in between, this book tells you those stories.

> ZACH ERTZ, Philadelphia Eagles Pro Bowl tight end

As a Bible ministry based in Philadelphia, we were thrilled to watch our courageous Eagles live out their faith and overcome the odds during an unforgettable run to the Super Bowl. *Birds of Pray* will inspire football fans and followers of Jesus to stand on the promises of God's Word when facing challenges and adversity in their own lives.

> DR. ROY L. PETERSON, President and CEO,
> American Bible Society

Rob Maaddi has been covering the Philadelphia Eagles for longer than I've been on the team. He has been on a faith journey with us and has witnessed our exploits both on and off the field. No one can tell the story better.

> COREY CLEMENT, Philadelphia Eagles running back

Inspiring, bold, and unforgettable—get to know the Philly spirit and Eagles' pride like never before in this book that details the faith of the Super Bowl champions.

BRANDON BROOKS, Philadelphia Eagles Pro Bowl
left guard

Looking for proof that faith and classic underdog grit can power you forward to victory? Look no further. *Birds of Pray* is exactly that.

LANE JOHNSON, Philadelphia Eagles All-Pro right tackle

Our team faced tremendous odds last year, and yet we overcame and went on to capture the Super Bowl title. The world knows the headline, but this book tells the inside story from someone—a fellow brother in Christ—who was with us the whole time. Don't miss it.

JORDAN HICKS, Philadelphia Eagles linebacker

As a member of the Eagles for some time, I was drawn to this team for their faith in the Lord and the support for one another. Rob has covered the Eagles for eighteen years. He was there nearly my entire career in Philadelphia. He knows the team, he understands their faith journey, and I know he knows the Lord. *Birds of Pray* is a unique look at what made the Eagles Super Bowl champs.

DAVID AKERS, Six-time Pro Bowl kicker

I cannot wait to get my hands on *Birds of Pray*. As a guy who has been part of those locker rooms and Bible studies and gameday morning church sessions, even I can say that this team was special and a little different in its approach. For all the great things they would individually and collectively accomplish, they made it very clear Jesus was going to be the beginning, middle, and end to every single thing they did. He would set the rhythm and heartbeat of all they did as players and everything would flow from that. Win or lose. Success or failure. As we all go through our own trials and difficulties, I'm excited to read how this Eagles team led by its quarterback with his own story of tribulation kept pointing to Jesus, no matter what.

DAN ORLOVSKY, Former NFL quarterback

BIRDS
OF PRAY

ALSO BY ROB MAADDI

Baseball Faith:
52 MLB Stars Reflect on Their Faith

Football Faith:
52 NFL Stars Reflect on Their Faith

Mike Schmidt:
The Phillies' Legendary Slugger

BIRDS OF PRAY

THE STORY OF THE PHILADELPHIA EAGLES' FAITH, BROTHERHOOD, AND SUPER BOWL VICTORY

ROB MAADDI

ZONDERVAN

Birds of Pray
Copyright © 2018 by Rob Maaddi

Requests for information should be addressed to:
Zondervan, *3900 Sparks Dr. SE, Grand Rapids, Michigan 49546*

ISBN 978-0-310-35585-4 (hardcover)

ISBN 978-0-310-35587-8 (audio)

ISBN 978-0-310-35586-1 (ebook)

Published in association with the literary agency of WordServe Literary Group, Ltd., www.wordserveliterary.com.

Cover design: Curt Diepenhorst
Cover photo: Michael Perez / ASSOCIATED PRESS
Interior design: Kait Lamphere
Photo insert background: istock/courtneyk

First printing June 2018 / Printed in the United States of America

*Thank you, Jesus, for making the ultimate sacrifice for
me and everyone. Thank you to my beautiful wife, Remy,
for your love, support, encouragement, and inspiring me to
be the best version of me. Thank you to my gorgeous daughters,
Alexia and Melina, for being the best daddy's girls. Thank you to
my parents, Issa and Hayat, for your unconditional love. Special
thanks to all the Philadelphia Eagles who openly and boldly
shared their faith with me. Congratulations to the team,
the entire organization, and all the passionate fans.*

But God demonstrates his own love for us in this:
While we were still sinners, Christ died for us.

ROMANS 5:8

CONTENTS

FOREWORD

Getting injured last season was extremely challenging. Ever since I was a kid, I had envisioned myself holding that Lombardi Trophy up on that stage in my uniform. Obviously, my season was cut short. I still believed we would do that as a team, but now I wouldn't be the guy up there. I had to swallow my pride and walk through that with God and really trust Him and his faithfulness. I truly believed that God was writing a different story and my reach would be so much more effective because of the hardships I was going through. My favorite thing about it was that at the end of the day, Jesus Christ took all of the glory through Nick Foles and Coach Doug Pederson on that stage.

In *Birds of Pray*, Rob Maaddi captures the story of our brotherhood and the special bond we have in Christ that helped us become Super Bowl champions.

There are things the world idolizes, like money and fame, but that's not what it's all about. I see a lot of guys who have so-called "everything" but truly have nothing. I believe everyone, inside of themselves, is longing for something. Money, fame, sports, and so many things can be an idol and fill that void, but they won't last. That void can only be permanently filled by having a personal relationship with Jesus Christ.

I challenge you to go to Him and to seek Him. The Bible says: "When you seek Him with all your heart, you will find Him." He will not only change your life here on earth, but He'll give you eternal rest with Him forever.

Carson Wentz

INTRODUCTION: FAN, FOLLOWER, DISCIPLE

I used to party with professional athletes. Now, I pray with them.

I began covering Philadelphia sports teams full-time in 2000. It was a dream job for a kid who grew up a few miles from the stadium complex in South Philly.

Since I was a kid, I've always been a diehard sports fan. Loved to watch and loved to play even more. Still do, though years of throwing my body around on baseball and football fields have taken a toll. I tore my left ACL after intercepting a pass in a touch football game. I tore thumb ligaments diving headfirst into second base in a college baseball game. The list is long.

I was reckless on the field, and for years I was even more reckless off it.

Partying with athletes in bars and nightclubs led me down the wrong path. I couldn't compete with pros at their sport. So I tried to compete with them where I could. It was all about hooking up with the most beautiful girls. I went from one unfaithful relationship to another, beginning with my first marriage. I was the ultimate womanizer and proud of it. I even justified my behavior, convincing myself that socializing with players would allow me to earn their trust and get big scoops. It takes hard work to break news, and I was willing to go above and beyond the job description. But while we were out, I spent more time chasing women than chasing stories.

I played wing man one night for a star player going into his free agency offseason after he promised I would get the first call the second he signed with a new team only to have his agent give the news to another reporter.

My partying paid off the time I was the only reporter celebrating future Hall of Fame receiver Terrell Owens's thirty-second birthday at Jay Z's 40/40 club in Atlantic City just a few weeks after T.O. was kicked off the Philadelphia Eagles in 2005. I got an exclusive that night thanks to the two girls who led me past security for the invitation-only event.

I saw things that would've filled a celebrity gossip column but never said a word. I honored the "guy code" and worked harder to preserve my relationships with athletes than saving my marriage.

I thought my wild lifestyle was under control. I didn't really drink alcohol. I never smoked anything or tried any drugs. I didn't go to strip clubs. Womanizing was my vice. And the whole time running around, I was a very religious guy. I prayed. I went to Mass. I sinned. I went to confession. I started over. The cycle repeated.

I even got four religious tattoos as if I could ink my way to heaven. The third one is a dove, the symbol for the Holy Spirit. It's inked on my right outer thigh surrounded by these words:

"Holy Spirit Guide Me." Looking back, I admit it was a cry for help. I got it a year after my divorce. My ex-wife said, "The Holy Spirit won't guide you if you don't let him." I've never forgotten those words. But I ignored that wisdom a little while longer.

I grew up in the church and went to Catholic schools for twelve years, so I knew all about Jesus. I was a big fan. But I didn't know Him personally.

I had a great life on the outside. Nice cars. Fantastic job. Beautiful house in New Jersey in a suburban neighborhood. Surrounded by gorgeous girls. I worked out religiously and invested a ton of time on my outward appearance because I was ugly inside. Deep down, my behavior bothered me. I was unfulfilled, never satisfied, always searching and seeking something else or someone new.

Finally, my life changed dramatically when I accepted Christ as my Lord and Savior on my third trip to Times Square Church in New York City on August 29, 2010. I heard the powerful testimony of a former drug dealer who said a cop took his stash during a raid, threw it out, and told him he was giving him a second chance. He ran off and never looked back, turned his life around, and became a minister.

The Holy Spirit had been tugging at my heart, and God had been placing people in my life who were planting seeds. That was the last push I needed. I answered the altar call that Sunday evening. I put my ego aside, walked down from the rafters of the amphitheater, and stood in the front of the church. With tears in my eyes and years of guilt in my heart, I invited Jesus into my life. I asked Him to help me overcome my problem and promised to take Him everywhere I went. I left that church with an overwhelming sense of peace that has never left me.

I went from being a fan of Jesus to being a follower that day. It was the best decision I ever made. I didn't leave Jesus at church anymore. I made Him Lord of all. I realized a relationship with Christ is more fulfilling than all the rules and rituals of religion that I had followed faithfully but left me broken.

My life didn't instantly become easier or better. Christianity isn't a magic pill. Problems don't disappear, and there are consequences for past actions, but Christ equips us with the armor to fight our inner and outer battles. I no longer had to fight on my own. I turned to Jesus to help me whenever temptation came, whenever the enemy attacked me, whenever I felt weak. I learned to avoid putting myself in situations that could lead me to fail. I started to surround myself with like-minded Christians who would encourage me in my walk rather than enablers who were bringing me down. I began to gravitate toward Christian players in the Eagles locker room to discuss Scripture instead of making plans to party.

A few years later, I joined the Deacons Prison Ministry softball team. We travel across several states to share the gospel with inmates. After sharing my testimony for the first time on a rainy afternoon at a prison in West Virginia on July 27, 2015, I knew God's plan for me. He turned my mess into His message. I was called to be a disciple. Spreading the gospel became my passion, and I've been on a mission to do everything I can to increase the kingdom, to inspire and enlighten nonbelievers, and encourage and challenge believers to dig deeper in their faith and move them toward action. I even took the unconventional road of starring in a reality television series with my wife, Remy, so we could use that platform to share Christ.

I met Remy six months after I came to Christ. She's the most beautiful person on the outside and the inside that I've ever known.

Remy had moved to Harrisburg, Pennsylvania, from Egypt with her family at age fifteen. She graduated from Penn State and was a social worker when we started dating. Ten months later, we got engaged. We had strong Christian backgrounds but were both early in our journey with the Lord. We grew together in love and in our walk with Christ. We overcame selfishness and materialistic attitudes. We built our relationship on the foundation of our faith. When the opportunity to do television arose, we embraced it because we wanted to tell the audience about Jesus. We didn't get a chance to do it directly on air, but the platform to share Christ with fans on social media has been tremendous. We were blessed with twin daughters in 2013. God has been working in our lives nonstop.

Meanwhile, my relationships with Christian athletes led me to write two books: *Football Faith* and *Baseball Faith*. That was only the beginning. I launched *Faith On The Field Show* on Philadelphia's 610 ESPN radio in April 2017 to give athletes a forum to discuss how God has impacted their lives and to use sports as a vehicle to share the message of Jesus.

The 2017 Philadelphia Eagles were a unique team of destiny led by a group of Christian men bound by their strong faith who sharpened each other, boldly proclaimed their love for Jesus, and played for an Audience of One. It was, and is, refreshing to witness their genuine love for Christ. I love their passion to make disciples.

They were Champions for Christ before they became Super Bowl champions.

I'm honored to tell their story in *Birds of Pray*.

CHAPTER ONE

SUPER BOWL MORNING

Eight and a half hours before kickoff for Super Bowl LII, members of the Philadelphia Eagles got ready for the biggest game of their lives with an intimate celebration of their love for Jesus Christ. About twenty players gathered in the offensive meeting room at the team hotel for a worship service organized by Carson Wentz and Trey Burton. The underdog Eagles were set to play against the defending champion New England Patriots, one victory from finally capturing that elusive Vince Lombardi Trophy for the first time in franchise history and bringing it home to a city starving for a National Football League title. But for the guys in that conference room and a few others on the team, their relationship with Jesus was more important than winning football games.

Wentz, the franchise quarterback who was on his way to likely winning the league's Most Valuable Player Award in only his second season before wrecking his left knee in Week 14, and Burton, the backup tight end who later that night would become a central figure in one of the greatest plays in sports history, had planned similar worship services over the past two seasons. Whenever the Eagles had free time on a Sunday morning because they were playing a game in late afternoon or at night, players held "church" at their hotel. It didn't matter if they were playing against the woeful Cleveland Browns in September or trying to prevent the Patriots from winning their sixth ring. Getting together to praise God was the top priority for these brothers in Christ. The stakes just happened to be much higher on this frigid Sunday morning in Minnesota.

"Given the obvious fact that we're not in church on Sundays, we're always looking for ways to implement that," Wentz told me a week after we did a faith event together at a Christian high school in New Jersey. I first asked him about Super Bowl morning on the limo ride home following that event. He didn't think it was extraordinary because it was something the team always did together. I insisted it was pretty special, so he was happy to share some details.

"We would always have chapel the night before, but some guys wouldn't always make it," he continued. "It's tough when you're on the road and you have plans if you're going out to dinner. So it's really cool to have our own form of church service for anyone who could make it. It's just normal for us. That was just what we did and what we knew."

Community worship was part of the daily fabric of this team, similar to studying the playbook, watching film, working out, and practicing. On Monday nights, players gathered with their significant others for Bible study at a teammate's house. On Thursday nights, they had Bible study for players at the practice facility with the team chaplain, Pastor Ted Winsley. On nights before games, they had a chapel service at the team hotel followed by prayer and fellowship in their rooms. Sometimes they had a guest speaker or musician. Before a Thursday night game against the Carolina Panthers in Week 6, Mack Brock, former lead singer for Elevation Worship, joined the players at the team hotel and led them in worship.

At the Super Bowl Sunday service, they spent the first thirty to-forty minutes watching videos of some of their favorite worship songs on the same projector screen used to watch game film during the week. Guys lifted their hands to the Lord, sang along to the powerful music, and focused their minds and hearts on what mattered most: serving their Savior, no matter what the outcome of the game.

Pastor Kyle Horner, founder of The Connect Church in Cherry Hill, New Jersey, followed with a fifteen-minute message of encouragement, reminding the players who God created them to be and how they could give Him glory. Horner, a former college quarterback at Tennessee and Richmond, has a strong relationship with several players who go to his church.

"They just love Jesus and this is what they do," Horner told me a few months later. "They're not using Jesus as a crutch. They're not coming just to get their religious fix on a Super Bowl morning. This is who they want to be, and they want to pray for their brothers and do this thing together. The power in it is them treating the Super Bowl just like any other game. They're not trying to get God on their side. They're not trying to do something to make God happy with them. Keeping God in the center of it all is who they are. That's what enabled them to play the way they played."

After Horner spoke, players broke into groups of two or three instead of their usual large prayer circle. They laid hands on and prayed over each other.

"I remember that being pretty cool that we got in small groups and prayed with and for each other out loud," Wentz said. "It keeps God in the middle of it and strengthens the community as well where we're not sitting there in church, listening, and leaving. We're doing this together. We're brothers in Christ, and that's bigger than each of us."

Pro Bowl tight end Zach Ertz, starting left guard Stefen Wisniewski, injured special teams captain Chris Maragos, injured star linebacker Jordan Hicks, and reserve wide receiver Marcus Johnson were among the players in the room that morning. Nick Foles couldn't be there because he was in a meeting going over the final preparations for the game.

"Brothers in Christ, no matter what's going on in your life, you have Jesus and you have each other, and that's never gonna change," Wisniewski had told me a few days before the game, when anticipation was running high. "God is with us no matter what, and if that's real to you because you're spending time with God every day, if that's real to you because you're spending time with your brothers in Christ, then no matter what you're going through, you can still have joy, you can still have peace, and you can be more than a conqueror of any of your circumstances. That definitely helped this team and all the Christians on this team to persevere."

Players were certainly excited to play against New England in the Super Bowl. To a man, every guy wanted to win, to take down Bill Belichick, Tom Brady, and the Patriots dynasty. Every kid dreams about winning a Super Bowl from the minute they step foot on a Pee Wee league field. These were big-time competitors playing on the grandest stage. They understood the significance of the game. But winning or losing the Super Bowl wasn't going to define this group of men on the Philadelphia Eagles. Their identity wasn't rooted in their accomplishments; it was found in Christ.

"Worshiping God is not what they do, it's who they are, and that's the difference between religion and what these guys have, and that's a relationship with Jesus," Horner said. "Who they are is building a lifestyle of worship for God whether on the field or off the field. I recognize in sports everybody has their own pregame ritual. For these guys, this service was more than that. It wasn't just a pregame ritual. This was an intentional act of love, devotion, and choosing God first. When you're talking about being on that platform, that level, the biggest platform ever, a billion people watching this game, it would've been easy for guys to skip it because they had chapel the night before. But for them, it was Sunday morning. This is who they are. This is what made the Eagles special."

CHAPTER TWO

THE REJECTED STONE

Howie Roseman became obsessed with football at age seven. Born in Brooklyn and raised in North Jersey, he dreamed of playing for the New York Jets. But he was a small kid, and his mom wouldn't even sign the permission slip to let him play in the Pee Wee league. That didn't dash his NFL hopes. Young Howie turned his attention to running a football team. He watched as many games as he could, read all the stories he could find—this was several years before the internet made everything easily available—and he took copious notes. Other kids were watching cartoons or playing games, but Roseman became the quintessential football geek. He was playing the long game—starting at seven years old.

"I would tell people that I wanted to be a general manager in the National Football League, and they would laugh at me," Roseman said. "I wouldn't say I'm the most spiritual person but there was something inside me that said this is what I'm going to do."

Roseman was determined to make his dream come true. He began sending letters to NFL teams seeking an internship during his senior year at Marlboro High School in New Jersey.

"I got rejected, rejected, rejected," he said.

In college, Roseman figured he could start his career in coaching and work his way up to a job in the front office. He chose the University of Florida because he loved the Gators football team. He applied for a position with the Gators and received a familiar response.

"Again, I was rejected, rejected, rejected," he recalled.

Roseman kept sending those letters to NFL teams, trying to get his foot in the door any way he could. When he received a rejection letter, he sent notes back saying "thanks."

Finally, during his senior year, someone noticed his persistence. Mike Tannenbaum, who was working in the Jets' front office, called Roseman to offer advice. He told him teams wouldn't hire someone with no experience to be a scout. He advised him to go to law school and market himself to teams as a salary-cap expert. So Roseman went to Fordham Law School. He continued his pursuit and sent more letters, adding his own scouting reports and individual breakdowns of players by positions. But rejections kept coming.

"I would've worked anywhere," he said. "I just wanted an opportunity, a summer internship. I would've worked for free."

Roseman was determined to reach his goal. He considered applying for a job in the short-lived XFL, a professional football league that was a joint venture between NBC and the World Wrestling Federation (now known as World Wrestling Entertainment). The league lasted only one season in 2001. But Tannenbaum called Roseman again, this time to interview him for an internship with the Jets.

"He said, 'Every three resumés, I see a copy of yours. And then after it, I see letters from you thanking me for rejecting you,'" Roseman said.

Roseman didn't get that internship, but Tannenbaum promised he'd recommend him to another team that had an opening. Roseman set his sights on the Eagles because they were close to home and began calling Joe Banner, who was the team president at the time. Banner called Tannenbaum to make sure Roseman wasn't a stalker and eventually offered him an unpaid summer internship in 2000. All that persistence had paid off. Roseman spent the next six months waking up at 4:15 every morning to catch a train from New York to Philadelphia. He'd return home late at night, get up, and do the same thing day after day. Roseman didn't have an office or even a desk in the old, dingy Veterans Stadium. Those train rides were adding up, and he was accumulating more debt instead of paying off student loans. But it was worth it because he was pursuing his dream.

After his internship, he was hired full-time as the team's salary-cap staff counsel. He moved to Philadelphia and dedicated himself to learning everything he could. Roseman spent all day in the office and then would join Bobby DePaul and Mike McCartney in the scouting department after he finished his regular duties. Management allowed him the freedom to learn whatever he could about talent evaluation. He began writing draft reports and grading pro players to help him assign cash value to guys. Three years later, Roseman was promoted to director of football administration. He was named vice president of football administration in 2006 and became vice president of player personnel two years later.

Over that time, Roseman accumulated valuable experience working on the salary cap, negotiating contracts, scouting pro players and college guys. He worked his way up the ranks until his dream came true on January 29, 2010. Roseman was named general manager of the Eagles, becoming the youngest person at age thirty-four to hold that position in the NFL.

Led by quarterback Michael Vick, who was two years removed from serving a prison sentence for his role in running a dogfighting operation, the Eagles won the NFC East title in Roseman's first season as general manager. But they lost to the Green Bay Packers in the first round of the playoffs. They missed the playoffs the next two seasons, and head coach Andy Reid was fired and replaced by Chip Kelly in 2013. Kelly guided the Eagles to a division title in his first season with Nick Foles leading the way at quarterback. But they lost another first-round playoff game—this time to the New Orleans Saints.

Roseman played an instrumental role in convincing Kelly to leave the successful college program he built at Oregon to coach in the NFL. But their relationship deteriorated over the first two years. It reached a point where team owner Jeffrey Lurie had to make a decision. He chose Kelly—temporarily. Lurie relieved Roseman of his duties as general manager on January 2, 2015. But, Roseman wasn't fired. He was "promoted" to executive vice president of football operations. However, Kelly was given control of personnel decisions while Roseman was exiled to a new office in a different part of the building. Kelly won the power struggle, but it didn't last long. The experiment was a disaster. Kelly's roster moves backfired, the team started losing, and he alienated some key players who didn't like his communication skills. Lane Johnson, one of the team's best offensive linemen, called Kelly a "brilliant coach" who allowed his ego to get in the way. Johnson also called Kelly more of a "dictator" than a coach.

Lurie abruptly fired Kelly with one game remaining in the 2015 season, ending a three-year stint that produced two winning seasons, one division championship, no playoff victories, and plenty of dysfunction in the organization.

Then Lurie put Roseman back in charge, expanding his role as the executive vice president to include control of personnel decisions once again. He gave him a directive to change the culture. Lurie's decision wasn't popular among fans and some media. Critics argued that Roseman wasn't a "football guy" because he didn't have a traditional background. He wasn't a former player or coach. He was viewed simply as a salary-cap guru who only knew how to crunch numbers and couldn't identify talented football players. The skeptics argued that he wasn't qualified to assemble a championship roster. But Lurie believed in Roseman and was willing to give him a second chance to run the team's football operations department. Roseman made the most of his one-year hiatus, seeking input from team leaders in other sports to help him understand what it takes to build a champion. The prevailing message he learned was that winning a championship requires more than simply acquiring the best players. Chemistry is vital to a team's success so Roseman was determined to build a team of people who had the same goal. He also learned to delegate authority.

"I was a young guy who had a lot of responsibility, and sometimes when you do that, you want to take more on your plate, and you want to feel like, 'I gotta make these decisions because this is the role,' but it's all about collaborating and getting people's point of view and then trying to make the best decision for the team," Roseman said.

Rejected numerous times before he overcame high odds to

land a job in the NFL, Roseman rebounded from more rejection after losing his dream job and regained power in the front office.

Like the stone the builders rejected in Psalm 118:22, Roseman ultimately became the one that became the cornerstone.

Lurie and Roseman now had to find a new head coach who could restore the family atmosphere they valued so much and instill a winning attitude. Lurie emphasized that one of the qualities he valued most in the next coach was "emotional intelligence." After an exhaustive search that began with a list of twenty-five candidates, the team hired Doug Pederson on January 18, 2016.

"A key ingredient for me, and I think when you go to this it kind of defines differences between candidates, and that is who is the most comfortable in their own skin," Lurie said after hiring Pederson. "And when I say that, what I mean is an ability to be genuine at all times. I got to spend a lot of time with our players at the beginning of this coaching search, and the message loud and clear, which I agree with in terms of leadership in today's world, no matter what, is that you've got to be comfortable in your own skin in order to be able to reach out, be genuine with those you want to get high performance from, be accountable to them, and make them accountable to you. When you get down to it, that's something that we were not going to go away from. That was a very key variable, and Doug has that unquestionably. I think what Doug brings also is an understanding of the passion of our fans in Philadelphia."

That passion is more than showing up with painted faces at the stadium on Sundays. Philly fans live and die with their sports teams every day. They're obsessed with winning. They're smart fans who understand the game but often think they know more than coaches, managers, and owners. They're quick to boo their own teams when they're losing or underachieving. But once Philly fans accept a guy as one of their own, it's a lifetime honeymoon.

Pederson was a familiar face who already had two stints with the Eagles—first as a player and then as an assistant coach. He spent the previous three seasons with the Kansas City Chiefs as the offensive coordinator on Andy Reid's staff. Pederson was a backup quarterback during most of his playing career, playing behind Hall of Famers Dan Marino and Brett Favre for several seasons. He earned a Super Bowl ring with Favre on the Packers and got his first chance to be a starter when Reid brought him from Green Bay to Philadelphia with him to mentor Donovan McNabb during his rookie season in 1999.

Pederson only played one year in Philly and spent five more seasons in the NFL, including the last four back in Green Bay. After retiring, he returned to Louisiana, where he went to college and began his coaching career at Calvary Baptist Academy, a private Christian high school in Shreveport. Pederson was there from 2005 to 2009 before Reid brought him back to the NFL and to Philadelphia to work as an assistant coach.

During his career in the NFL, Pederson played for Reid and legendary coaches Don Shula and Mike Holmgren. He learned from some of the best in the sport and obviously impressed Lurie and Roseman with his football knowledge. Lurie called Pederson a "smart, strategic thinker" who, when he mentored other young quarterbacks during his playing career, showed signs that he would be a future coach.

But Pederson's resumé didn't impress many Eagles fans and some of the media, of course. Several talk-show hosts on Philadelphia's sports radio stations criticized the decision to hire Pederson. Newspaper reporters and columnists questioned his qualifications. Pederson was viewed as a less-qualified version of Reid, who was maligned for his failure to win a championship during fourteen seasons in Philadelphia. Reid won more games than any coach in franchise history. He guided the Eagles to 120 wins in the regular season, 10 wins in the playoffs, six division titles and five appearances in the conference championship game. But the Eagles lost to the New England Patriots in their only Super Bowl appearance under his direction.

That wasn't good enough in a football-crazed town filled with a rabid base of blue-collar, diehard fans who desperately wanted to win a Super Bowl. Philadelphia sports fans are passionate and intelligent, but sometimes they misbehave. They have an overblown reputation for rowdy behavior, mostly because the national media harps on an infamous moment when Eagles fans tossed snowballs at Santa Claus in 1968. There were circumstances surrounding the incident that people often ignore, however. The man wearing the costume was a fill-in Santa sitting in the crowd, and some in attendance have questioned the condition of his suit as well as his sobriety. Plus, fans were already upset with a team that was on its way to losing its final game to finish 2–12. So they took it out on poor Santa. Fans in other cities have also behaved badly in stadiums across the country. There's been violence in several other cities, but Philadelphia gets a bad rap for the Santa incident.

Fans in Philly love the Phillies, Flyers, and 76ers. But the Eagles, or Iggles as the old-timers say, are number one in the City of Brotherly Love.

The Eagles hadn't won a championship since defeating Vince Lombardi's Packers in the 1960 title game. Reid couldn't deliver a Super Bowl victory, and critics were certain his protégé—Pederson—would never win one either.

Lurie, Roseman, and Pederson agreed the team needed a franchise quarterback to build around, even though the Eagles already had re-signed Sam Bradford to a two-year contract worth $36 million. Jared Goff and Carson Wentz were projected to be the two best college quarterbacks in the 2016 NFL draft. But the Eagles had the thirteenth pick so Roseman had to find a way to move up. He deftly maneuvered from No. 13 to No. 8 to No. 2 by trading three players Kelly had acquired the previous offseason—running back DeMarco Murray, linebacker Kiko Alonso, and cornerback Byron Maxwell—and five draft picks.

Roseman's top target was Wentz, who led North Dakota State to consecutive Football Championship Subdivision national titles in his final two collegiate seasons. Wentz had all the measurables scouts desire in a big-time quarterback—size, arm strength, mobility. The only knock against him was the level of competition he faced. But the Eagles were convinced Wentz could be an elite quarterback in the pros. After the Los Angeles Rams selected Goff with the first pick, the Eagles got their man. Wentz became the highest selection ever for an FCS player.

"One player can change your team, and for us, we know how important that is, that position, and so investing in that position was a no-brainer," Roseman said after choosing Wentz. "When you talk about Carson, you're talking about a blue-collar quarterback.

This guy has incredible work ethic. He's got incredible passion. He fits into this city, into the personality of this city, and you see that when he plays. He plays with that passion. He takes the city and team on its back, and that's what he'll do the minute he steps in here, and it's infectious. All of us when we're around him, you want to be around him more because he has that energy and that desire to be great and to win."

With Howie Roseman calling the shots, Doug Pederson coaching the team, and Carson Wentz in the fold, a new era for the Philadelphia Eagles had begun.

CHAPTER
THREE

TAKE ME TO THE WATER

Six weeks into the 2016 season, the Philadelphia Eagles were an enigma. They won the first three games, a surprising start considering they had a rookie head coach and a rookie quarterback. Fans overreacted, naturally, and started thinking about the playoffs. But the Eagles lost their next two games after an early bye week slowed their momentum, and they were looking more like the rebuilding team everyone expected at the start. Experts had predicted the Eagles would win between six and eight games. Optimists figured the playoffs were a year away.

It takes time to build a champion-caliber roster in the NFL, and the Eagles were starting fresh with a new organizational structure, new coaching staff, and new quarterback. Even Bill Belichick had a losing record (5–11) in his first season in New England, though he won the first of five Super Bowl titles with the Patriots the following year. Realistically, this was a prove-it season for the Eagles. If Carson Wentz proved he was indeed a franchise quarterback worth all the draft picks the Eagles traded away to get him, and if Doug Pederson proved he was the right coach for the team, it would be a successful season regardless of wins and losses.

———————

While the team showed inconsistency on the field through the first five games, there was something powerful happening inside the locker room. Players were bonding over their love for Jesus. They were uplifting each other, encouraging each other, inspiring each other. Together, a group of Christian players were seeking a deeper understanding of Scripture and a stronger relationship with the Lord. Philadelphia is a tough town with a tough media contingent. But listening to the players answer questions and watching the way they conducted their business, it was clear this was a special group of men. Many players expressed their faith on social media by posting Bible verses and inspirational Christian messages. Anyone can publicly profess to be a Christian, but the players on this team walked their talk.

"That season was when a core group of believers dedicated themselves to Christ, to the organization, and to one another," said Pastor Ted Winsley, the team chaplain. "It was really when it clicked for them that football is not our purpose; it's a platform, and it's our responsibility to use it for His glory."

Winsley, founder of The Family Church in Voorhees, New Jersey, began his volunteer role with the team in 2002 after being invited by Troy Vincent, a former All-Pro cornerback with the Eagles and the NFL's executive vice president of football operations since 2014. Built like a linebacker, Winsley relates well to the players. "I'm a pastor. You put me in a room with men, that's what I'm gonna do. I do it with a special people group that need it desperately," he said.

Players took this time seriously, just as they took their game seriously. They met often during the week for Bible studies, devotionals, prayer, and fellowship.

"It's an accountability time where guys get to sharpen each other," special-teams ace Chris Maragos said. "As a veteran, I get to impart wisdom to the younger guys. They get to feed into the older guys. We learn from each other and grow a little bit."

Trey Burton noticed more players were coming to these prayer meetings. Burton, who joined the team as an undrafted free agent in 2014 after four years at the University of Florida, had become one of the spiritual leaders on the team. He approached Winsley early in the season with an idea to offer baptism.

"We wanted to make sure all the guys coming to Bible study who had accepted Christ or made a new dedication to the Lord had an opportunity to be baptized," Burton said. "We don't get to go to church on Sunday during the season so we have our own little church at the facility, and I remember praying about it, and I went up to Ted and said: 'I really think we need to give guys an opportunity to be baptized.' He thought it was a great idea, and he started a lesson on baptism, what it means and why do we get baptized."

Burton was a star quarterback in high school in Venice, Florida, and was recruited by former Gators coach Urban Meyer. As a freshman in 2010, Burton broke Tim Tebow's school record for touchdowns in a game by scoring six in a 48–14 victory over Kentucky. He had five rushing and one receiving. But Burton later called it "probably the worst thing that happened to me in my entire life" because he wasn't strong in his faith at the time and he wasn't prepared to handle all the attention he received after that game.

"I was religious, but I didn't have a relationship with the Lord," he said. "I was checking the boxes off, going to church, going to Bible study, praying occasionally, and a majority of the prayers would be that I would do good Saturday night or whenever I played."

Many people, not just athletes, use prayer to ask God for help achieving something whether it's in sports or life. It's important to be thankful for everything we already have and to appreciate all our blessings, especially the ones we take for granted. Thanking God for everything before asking Him for anything is a great way to start our daily prayer. Besides, turning to God only in times of need isn't the way a relationship with Him is supposed to work. Going to someone only when we want something is not a recipe for a healthy relationship.

"I was using the Lord as a rabbit's foot or a lucky charm," Burton explained. "So after that game, breaking Tebow's record, a lot of publicity, a lot of people wanting to take pictures and wanting to meet me, it caused a downward spiral in my life, caused me to go down the wrong path. I started to do things that really were ridiculous and people shouldn't experience. It was a dark time in my life, and it led me to the point my sophomore year where I wanted to quit football and never play again. Ultimately, it led to my girlfriend being pregnant and me being one of the Christian figures, one of the godly figures on the team, sitting here with a pregnant girlfriend when I'm supposed to be Christian and not supposed to be having premarital sex. I'm walking this line with one foot in and one foot out, trying to live worldly and trying to live for God. It broke us. We were at rock bottom, and it wasn't until my junior year when my wife and I, separately and together, committed our lives to Christ."

Following his conversation with Burton about baptism, Winsley spent three weeks preaching to the players on identifying with water conversion and how baptism is a sign of transformation. Baptism doesn't make us Christians or give us an exclusive membership to become part of God's family, he explained. Rather, it shows we are part of God's family. Baptism is a public expression of faith. Jesus called it the first step of obedience, an outward expression of our commitment to God.

At the end of his series, Winsley offered the players an opportunity to be baptized. Jordan Hicks and fellow linebacker Kamu Grugier-Hill raised their hands. All they needed was a pool.

"The guys were hungry about wanting their lives changed," Winsley said. "Trey said, 'C'mon man, let's go in the cold tub.' And I was like, 'Can we do this?' Next thing I know we're in the cold tub and five players received Christ."

Approximately fifteen players gathered around the recovery pool at the team's practice facility on October 20, 2016, for one of the most unique events ever held at an NFL team's headquarters. The video that soon went viral shows it was truly an emotional experience for players. A group of players coming together in an odd setting for a powerful ceremony usually reserved for churches was quite special.

"It was surreal," Winsley said.

Athletes often use cold-water therapy to help their bodies recover from injuries and allow their fatigued muscles to recuperate from exercise, practice, and games. That night, the Eagles used the cold tub for a greater purpose. Instead of physical healing, it became a place for spiritual renewal and revival.

Burton, wearing a white short-sleeve shirt with an Eagles logo in the center, and Winsley, wearing a green short-sleeve shirt with *Eagles* written across the front, stood in the pool while the players sang "Take Me to the Water." Grugier-Hill, wearing a black, long-sleeve shirt with *Eagles* written across the front, stood in the middle with his arms folded across his chest. Winsley began the ceremony with a question: "Kamu, have you received Jesus Christ as your personal Lord and Savior?"

Grugier-Hill replied, "Yes."

Winsley said, "Then we baptize you in the name of the Father, the Son, and the Holy Spirit in the name of Jesus." Burton and Winsley dunked Grugier-Hill in the water and pulled him up as the guys cheered like a teammate had scored a touchdown.

Grugier-Hill, a rookie, was one of the newest guys on the team. He grew up in Hawaii, went to Eastern Illinois University, and was selected by New England in the sixth round of the draft. He was released at the end of training camp and immediately signed a contract with the Eagles one day later. The Patriots wound up winning the Super Bowl that season, but Grugier-Hill had no regrets missing out. God had another plan for him. His new teammates helped him grow closer to Jesus.

"Coming to the Eagles, the group we have is surrounded with Christ, it was such an amazing, eye-opening thing for me," Grugier-Hill said. "I grew up in a Christian house. I was baptized Catholic, but it was never really my faith; it was my mom's faith I was living off of. So when I had the opportunity to get baptized, I took it because I wanted to step out and proclaim my own faith for Jesus Christ."

Grugier-Hill said the most important lesson he has learned is that salvation is earned through God's grace, not by our good works.

"That's the biggest thing I had to learn because we're all sinners," Grugier-Hill said. "When I do something wrong, I feel so bad. I feel so convicted all the time. There's a fine line. You don't have to feel like that because God's grace is so awesome. You're saved. He loves you. He sent his son Jesus Christ to take care of your sins for you. At the same time, the fine line is you want to do good works for Him because of your faith."

The apostle Paul made that point clear in Ephesians 2:8–9. He wrote: "For it is by grace you have been saved, through faith—and this is not from yourselves, it is the gift of God—not by works, so that no one can boast."

Hicks entered the cold tub after Grugier-Hill walked out. "It was freezing," he said. Hicks was in his second season with the team and had already developed into one of the league's best playmakers at his position. Wearing a white short-sleeve shirt with an Eagles logo in the center, he got baptized and walked out of the water smiling and clapping. Raised by a single mom whose father was a preacher, Hicks was surrounded by people who influenced his faith from a young age. But he didn't always go to church.

"I was a mixed kid, and my sister is 100 percent white," Hicks said. "We had a tough time in the church. My mom would try to get us to go, but I was a holiday kid. I went Easter Sunday and Christmas. But someone was always present in my life. God planted seeds at every point."

Hicks moved with his family to Cincinnati when he was in the sixth grade. They went to live near an uncle who became one of his spiritual mentors.

"He was able to speak truth into me a little bit," Hicks said.

But when he moved away to college to play football at the University of Texas, Hicks began to veer down a different path.

"I didn't really believe in the relationship [with Christ] and I was living this sinful life and always looking to satisfy the flesh in so many different ways whether it was alcohol, women, or whatever it is, and it was never satisfying, not one time," Hicks said. "And I always knew there was something missing, but I could never figure it out."

Some of his Longhorns teammates took Hicks to Bible studies, chapel services, and Fellowship of Christian Athletes events. But he was still struggling in his faith when the Eagles selected him in the third round of the 2015 draft.

"I was still running, but my knowledge of who Christ was started to grow," Hicks said. "I met my wife in my last year in college, and she's one of the best people I ever met, and she influenced me a lot. And then I get to the Eagles, and the day that I got drafted, my uncle contacted Pastor Ted and said, 'You need to keep an eye on this guy.' My first year, I ran. I'd go to Bible study, and then I'd take off. I didn't want to be there."

Hicks was still too comfortable living worldly. He wasn't ready to make drastic changes. But the Christian culture surrounding him in the locker room drew him in. His relationship with his girlfriend was getting serious. He recognized a marriage built on the foundation of Christ was important.

"I knew I was gonna get engaged, and I knew nothing else had ever worked. I went to Pastor Ted and said, 'I've been running. I'm here.' And it was a few months later I got baptized in that pool. It's been a journey since. Life hasn't gotten easier. It's actually been harder, but that's what we're called to do. We're called to be tough most times and have a foundation set in Christ, and I've been so blessed to have so many people in my life to have spoken truth into my life."

After Hicks left the pool, Winsley and Burton started to exit.

"We just thought two of them were gonna be baptized. We were done," Winsley said.

But then linebacker Mychal Kendricks entered the pool to publicly profess his commitment to the Lord. Kendricks had become known as a ladies man a couple years earlier after pop music star Rihanna posted a picture of him on Instagram with a "MCM" caption that stands for "Man Crush Monday." Kendricks didn't attend the weekly Bible studies. He once told me he didn't read the Bible because it was difficult to understand. I told him I felt the same until my brother bought me the New Living Translation life application study version as a Christmas gift. I promised to get him one but didn't deliver.

"Of all the players, Mychal was the last one I expected to walk into that pool," Winsley said. "I didn't know he was in the crowd."

But Kendricks had already accepted Christ a month earlier in the basement of Winsley's house. Two days before the first game against the Cleveland Browns, Burton injured his calf in practice. Trainers told him he would likely be on the sideline for one month because of the severity of the injury. The Eagles quickly signed linebacker Najee Goode to replace Burton on special teams. Burton knew he needed to get back on the field quickly. He's a strong believer in the healing power of prayer and there is no injury God cannot handle.

"I get a call from Trey," Winsley recounted. "He told me, 'I tore my calf and I need you to lay hands.' He called me like I was a trainer, but I heard his faith. I went over to his house. His leg was in a boot. His wife and kids were waiting there, and we all laid hands and we prayed."

It worked. Burton said he instantly felt better after Winsley prayed over him. It wasn't a magic act, rather an act of faith. Burton only missed one game before returning to the field.

Kendricks had suffered a similar injury to his calf in the first game. After witnessing Burton's rapid recovery, he called Winsley.

Kendricks: "Yo, man, it's real."

Winsley: "What's real?"

Kendricks: "What happened to Trey."

Winsley: "What are you talking about?"

Kendricks: "I tore my calf just like Trey did. I'm sitting on the trainer's table, and next day Trey's running around, and there's nothing wrong with him. I said to him, 'What shot did you get?' And he said, 'Pastor Ted prayed for me, and the Lord healed me.' I'm coming over."

Kendricks arrived at Winsley's house within an hour. Forty-five minutes later, he surrendered his life to Christ.

"I explained to him you're not here for something physical; this isn't magic," Winsley said. "Trey trusted God, and he trusted God because he has a relationship with Him."

Everyone was smiling and clapping when Kendricks, wearing a gray, sleeveless shirt with an Eagles logo, got dunked in the water. Winsley and Burton again started to exit but turned back around when wide receiver Paul Turner walked into the pool next. Wide receiver David Watford followed him.

"It was really an unbelievable moment," Burton said. "It was cool on many sides. We were at the team facility. I don't know if anybody has been baptized at an NFL team's facility, and it was really cool that the pool they were getting baptized in is the same pool a majority of the players on the team go to for healing."

The players went from the pool to the locker room and gathered around for a Bible study. Winsley preached to them about commitment and adversity.

"Water baptism means you are committed, dedicated, and now you are identifying yourself as being with Christ, and when you do that, you're setting yourself apart, and that action is a declaration of war on the enemy," Winsley said.

Three days later, the Eagles beat Minnesota 21–10, handing the Vikings and quarterback Sam Bradford their first loss of the season. But tough times were coming. The Eagles lost seven of the next eight games and finished the season in last place in the NFC East with a 7–9 record.

Despite all the losing, the seeds for Philadelphia's championship run in 2017 were planted because many players were united by their Christian faith, and they formed a strong brotherhood that helped them overcome adversity and tremendous odds on the way to capturing the team's first Super Bowl title.

"There was a conversation among the players where they said to each other, 'It's time to go to the next level, to dedicate ourselves to this lifestyle,'" Winsley said.

CHAPTER FOUR

AUDIENCE OF ONE

When Carson Wentz runs out of the tunnel at Lincoln Financial Field, he hears seventy thousand screaming fans, but he's focused on playing for one: Jesus.

Tattooed on his right wrist are two letters and a number—*AO1*—that represent who he is and what he's all about. AO1 stands for "Audience of One," a motto that became the name for Wentz's charity foundation and inspired teammates to join him in his quest to glorify God and use their platform to spread the gospel.

Wentz, who grew up in the Lutheran church, adopted the phrase during his freshman year at North Dakota State where he began to grow spiritually after senior quarterback Dante Perez approached him at a practice to talk about the Bible.

"I'll never forget the day. We were stretching and my head was spinning, trying to learn the offensive playbook, and he goes, 'Hey, bro, have you ever read the Bible.' And I said, 'C'mon, bro. We're at practice,'" Wentz recalled. "At the time, though, I was searching, so when he said that, it struck a chord with me. We ended up meeting once a week for the whole year, and I read the entire New Testament my first year in college. My view of Christianity was basically flipped on its head."

AO1 became a way of life for the talented, ginger-haired quarterback who was hailed as the savior of the Philadelphia Eagles when he was drafted.

"It's more than just a nice, little, cute slogan; it's more than a logo. It's really part of everyday life for me," Wentz said. "Am I perfect? By no means. But it's just living, playing with that bigger perspective of doing it for the Lord. We can tell you how cool it is to play in front of seventy thousand fans and running out of that tunnel and the excitement that it brings, but at the end of the day, we're not playing for the fans, we're not playing for the media. First and foremost, we are playing to please the Lord and to bring Him honor and praise. And that's really what it's all about.

"For me also, it's not just playing, it's literally everything I do whether I'm with my friends, whether I'm driving home, eating dinner. Colossians 3:23 says 'Whatever you do, work at it with all your heart, as working for the Lord, not for human masters' and so that's just been kind of my life motto. Whatever it is I'm doing, I'm just going to work my tail off for it, but I just always have to keep my heart in check and make sure I'm working for the Lord first and foremost, and that's really been my motivating factor that's got me to this point."

Before the Eagles made the blockbuster trade with the Cleveland Browns to move up to the No. 2 spot in the 2016 NFL draft and possibly have a chance at selecting Wentz, scouts and team executives made sure they were comfortable investing their future in a kid very few schools wanted when he came out of high school. Wentz was a late-bloomer who grew from 5-foot-8 as a freshman to 6-foot-5 by his senior year at Century High School in Bismarck, North Dakota. He didn't play quarterback as a junior because of injuries and wasn't recruited by many colleges. Central Michigan was the only FBS-level school to express interest in Wentz, but he decided to stay close to home and play for the Bison. At North Dakota State, he excelled in a complex, pro-style offense. Wentz impressed talent evaluators in the Senior Bowl and at the NFL combine, dispelling the notion that he was just a small-school star feasting on sublevel talent.

His physical skills were obvious—strong arm, athletic, elusive. But his intangibles set him apart. Everyone who met Wentz raved about his character, poise, professionalism, and leadership.

"I think it was from the first time we met him at the Senior Bowl. He was just an incredibly impressive guy," Howie Roseman said. "His presence when he walks in the room, when he talks to you not only about football but about life, and then when you watch him interact with people, he walks in the restaurant, just the impressions people have. It was an interesting moment because we walked in the restaurant and I had to step out for a second, and when I walked back in, I saw the manager and the hostess talking to each other and saying, 'Carson is just the greatest guy. He's always so humble, and he's always so appreciative of all of us here.' They didn't know what we were doing, and it was just that's the kind of kid he is."

Roseman, Jeffrey Lurie, and Doug Pederson were convinced Wentz would be the right pick, the centerpiece to build the franchise's foundation around.

"He's a winner," Pederson said. "His demeanor, his aggressiveness, his willingness to learn, sharp kid, really was a very attractive pick for us and a very good fit for us."

Wentz wasn't expected to play much as a rookie because Sam

Bradford was being paid big bucks to start and Chase Daniel had signed a three-year contract worth $21 million to be the backup.

Pederson didn't even plan to have Wentz in uniform when the team played because it's standard for the third-string quarterback to be on the inactive list on game days. With Bradford and Daniel serving as mentors, the plan was to ease Wentz into the starting job the same way Pederson helped prepare Donovan McNabb in 1999.

Everything changed eight days before the season opener when Philadelphia traded Bradford to Minnesota to regain a first-round pick in the 2017 draft. Pederson named Wentz the starter instead of Daniel, even though the rookie missed the final three preseason games because of a fractured rib. Wentz was that impressive in practice.

"Just watching him in person throw the ball, just kind of some of the 'wow factor' throws that he makes from unconventional positions, you just kind of go, 'This guy's going to be special,'" Pederson said.

Wentz was sensational the first month of the season, leading the Eagles to wins in his first three games. He had some tough stretches in the middle half of the season as the team lost nine of its next eleven games. But he finished strong in the final two games—wins over the playoff-bound New York Giants and Dallas Cowboys. Wentz became the first Eagles quarterback to start all sixteen games since McNabb in 2008. He set an NFL rookie record and franchise record with 379 complete passes and established himself as the leader for the team. It was evident to everyone who saw him on a daily basis that his faith defined him. Wentz walked his talk. He put Christ first in his life, treated people respectfully, was humble, and wasn't afraid to use his platform to spread the gospel. Several of his teammates began to follow Wentz's AO1 philosophy.

"He doesn't play for you, he doesn't play for his parents, he doesn't play for me," former teammate Jordan Matthews said after the Eagles crushed the Pittsburgh Steelers, 34–3, in Week 3. "He plays for God straight up. So when you do that, there is no pressure. It is just straight up. He puts himself in a position where he doesn't have to put pressure on himself. He plays for God, and that makes it that much easier on him."

Wentz had a special opportunity to share the AO1 message on his cleats when the NFL held its inaugural "My Cause, My Cleats campaign" during Week 13 of his rookie season. The league gave players the chance to share the causes that are important to them by allowing them to put special designs on their cleats. More than five hundred players participated in the campaign.

Several Eagles wore custom-designed cleats with *AO1* written on one side—the *O* was a crown of thorns with a cross inside. Next to the slogan was a picture of an empty grave with three crosses above it. On the inside of the cleats was written "Romans 5:8." The Bible verse says, "But God demonstrates his own love for us in this: While we were still sinners, Christ died for us."

Wentz, Matthews, Chris Maragos, Jordan Hicks, and Kamu Grugier-Hill were among the players who wore those cleats.

"Being in the NFL, it's a big stage," Wentz said. "Playing in Philadelphia, I have a lot of eyes on me. I want to do my best to take the eyes off me and redirect them toward Jesus."

Even though the Eagles didn't make the playoffs in 2016, there was excitement for the future. Wentz proved the team's huge investment in him was worth it. Coaches, teammates, and fans were confident Wentz had what it takes to lead Philadelphia to a Super Bowl.

On the sideline New Year's Day during the final game of the regular season against the Cowboys, Wentz shook teammate Fletcher Cox's hand and said, "Next year, we go."

His words were prophetic.

Wentz is a fierce competitor who hates to lose whether he's playing football or playing any kind of game with teammates. He was determined to lead the Eagles to a championship. Wentz went to Houston for Super Bowl week and had a chance to experience the media frenzy surrounding the biggest sporting event in America.

"Being here makes me hungrier to get back as a participant," he said.

Wentz took a month off from throwing a football and enjoyed some time off by going hunting in New Zealand and hanging out with his dogs. He's an avid hunter and dog lover—Wentz's golden retriever Henley gave birth to eight puppies late in his rookie season so he had nine dogs in his house for a month until he gave seven away. He kept one and named him Jersey. He hosted the Eagles' offensive linemen at his house for a barbecue. He organized a trip with his receivers to North Dakota so they could run routes, catch passes, and bond over bison burgers.

In May, Wentz and Matthews joined Mission of Hope and a team led by Pastor Kyle Horner on a trip to Haiti. They painted a house together with people in the village, played soccer with kids, and talked about Jesus. It was a life-changing experience for Wentz, who returned to the United States with an even stronger desire to spread the gospel.

"Going to Haiti was incredible," Wentz said. "We only went

for three days, and you know everyone always goes on these missions trips and [thinks] I'm going to go change the culture and go make a difference there. It's an incredible thing and an incredible opportunity, but what really happens is it changes you. It changes your heart, it changes your life, it changes your perspective in a big way. This was my first mission trip, my first eye-opening event like this in my life.

"Going there, you could just see how much need there was physically. They had literally nothing. There was garbage lying in the streets; you could smell it. It was hotter than a son-of-a-gun over there, and they're living in these huts. There's no air conditioning, there's no bathrooms, like they are just struggling to get water. It was unbelievable, but what they had was joy; they had real joy. They interacted with people and had real community. It was just really challenging for me in that sense because we have so much stuff. I mean, my goodness, the life we live we are just surrounded by stuff everywhere we look, but do we have real joy? Do we have real community with our friends and our families? Another big thing for me that really kind of rocked me was going over there—we did this mission trip and we get over there, we fly all the way across the ocean, get to Haiti, a Third World country, to tell people about Jesus. And I'm sitting here, and we're talking about Jesus and telling them the gospel, and it's incredible. But at the end of the night I'm like, 'Okay, that was a really cool day, but why the heck did I have to come all the way over here to tell people about Jesus when I can barely do it to my neighbor?' I can barely turn in my locker and tell people about the Good News and so it was really challenging for me. I came back with this new perspective on really living intentionally, being on a mission for the Lord. That's something we always talk about on the team, being on a mission, being on a mission in everything you do. When I got to see that firsthand, it really changed my perspective."

After returning home, Wentz had an opportunity to preach at two churches in North Dakota. His sermons centered on explaining the difference between the notion that believers are saved by works versus the biblical truth that believers are saved by grace.

Wentz explained why he chose to deliver this important message.

"Being saved by works is obviously a lie, but it's a lie that a lot of people believe. It's a lie just in our culture," Wentz said. "I know for me as a man, even when I was a kid, with sports and anything I did, I was going to work my tail off to earn what I got. That's how I was wired, that's how the world kind of instills this value so to speak is work, work, work, and earn it. And that's kind of what I thought. I'd pray, I'd go to church, I'd do this and that, and I'm like that's great, I'm a good person, I did the right things and so I'm going to be saved naturally, right? That's what I thought. That's the lie that the devil wants you to believe.

"This verse really kind of changes that perspective. Ephesians 2:8–10—'For it is by grace you have been saved, through faith—and this is not from yourselves, it is a gift from God—not by works, so that no one can boast. For we are God's handiwork, created in Christ Jesus to do good works, which God prepared in advance for us to do.' So when I learned about this grace, my view of Christianity was really just flipped on its head. Christianity is the only religion in the world that you can't earn heaven, you can't earn an afterlife, you can't earn reincarnation or whatever it is that other people believe. Christianity says it's done; Jesus already did it. He took it all for you and this is what Paul is saying here in Ephesians. He's saying it's by grace alone you've been saved, not by works so that no one can boast. I mean he can't lay it out much clearer. Then he says: 'But we are God's handiwork, created in Christ Jesus to do good works.' See we're not saved by our actions, but our actions come out of our faith. I think it's a misconception that a lot of people have, and it's just an ultimate full surrender that I cannot do it on my own. I cannot earn any of it. We get caught up in doing good, doing good, doing good, that it's a daily thing for me to just remind myself: without Jesus in it, I can't do it. I can't earn my way to heaven and nobody can."

Wentz went back to North Dakota in July before training camp opened to launch "The Carson Wentz AO1 Foundation." Its goal is to "demonstrate the love of God by providing opportunities and support for the less fortunate and those in need."

The foundation has three main objectives that reflect some of Wentz's deepest passions: faith, the outdoors, and dogs. AO1 provides service dogs to assist individuals with their development and quality of life. It provides hunting, fishing, and outdoor opportunities for individuals with life-threatening illnesses, physical challenges, the underserved, or United States veterans. It also cares for and provides food, shelter, and educational opportunities for the underprivileged living in the United States and abroad.

"Throughout college, after I had given my life to Christ, I knew how important it was to give back and help people," Wentz said. "Everybody else in my world was telling me to wait, take my time, take a few years, get established in the NFL, and I'd look at them and ask why? They didn't have an answer for me. Those are valuable years to use the platform God has given me to give back. The Lord put it on my heart a long time ago, and it's been in the making for quite some time. All the support has blown my mind.

God has done amazing things through it, and it's continuing to grow. It's an amazing opportunity for me to point people to Him."

Wentz returned to Haiti in April 2018 with Horner, Zach Ertz, third-string quarterback Nate Sudfeld, and wide receiver Rashard Davis. He launched plans to build a sports complex in the country and a month later pledged to match up to $500,000 for every dollar donated for it during a two-week fundraising campaign. Several weeks later, twenty-five thousand fans came out to see the inaugural Carson Wentz AO1 Foundation charity softball game and home run derby at Citizens Bank Park, home of the Philadelphia Phillies. Wentz's teammates played an entertaining game while he coached one team and Jordan Hicks coached the other. More than $850,000 was raised that night. Wentz had to sit out the softball action because he was still rehabbing from knee surgery, although he was on the field ahead of schedule with his teammates for seven-on-seven drills during organized team activities a few days later.

"Everything we do is to spread the gospel and make disciples of Jesus and we do it through different programs and different ways to provide physical need and opportunities," Wentz said.

Wentz's willingness to boldly proclaim his faith drew plenty of attention in Philadelphia during his first offseason when there wasn't much to talk about on sports radio stations because the Phillies weren't playing well and the Flyers and 76ers didn't make the playoffs. The Eagles usually dominate the conversation on the airwaves twelve months a year. One of the all-sports radio stations in Philadelphia dedicated more than one day of conversation debating whether it's appropriate for the quarterback of the Eagles to proclaim his Christian beliefs on social media. A Bible verse that Wentz posted on Twitter during Memorial Day weekend sparked the debate. Wentz posted: 1 Peter 5:8–9: "Be alert and of sober mind. Your enemy the devil prowls around like a roaring lion looking for someone to devour. Resist him."

One of the hosts misinterpreted the verse, thinking "sober" was a reference to alcohol. He said he didn't want his favorite team's quarterback to tell him he shouldn't drink beer on a holiday. The verse actually warns believers to watch out for Satan's attacks when we're suffering, feeling alone, or weak because that's when we're most susceptible. Wentz was undeterred by the misguided folks who criticized him for sharing his love for Jesus.

"If you're living in the world, yeah, it's hard, it's really hard," Wentz said about ignoring the critics. "But if you're rooted in the Word, it's not. In the world we live in, with freedom of speech and social media, everyone has their opinion and everyone has a bold opinion behind a screen.

"But we have the greatest example, and that's Jesus. Jesus was persecuted everywhere He went. Jesus was murdered on a cross. It doesn't get much worse than that. In that day and age, it doesn't get any more humiliating and embarrassing than that, and so if Jesus, who is our ultimate example, endured that, then I can endure a couple tweets, I can endure a little verbal abuse. I can keep that out and stay true to His Word because at the end of the day, I can stay true to that, and Jesus is ultimately the example.

"And then there's tons of people in the [Bible], you just read through Acts and there's names and things people were doing. Paul was told 'you're going to go to jail if you talk about Jesus.' Paul says, 'Well okay, Jesus did this, this, and this.' [Paul was told]: 'All right, you're in jail, bro.' I mean this is what he did; he was just bold because he knew the truth. If you love something enough, you're going to talk about it. If you love your wife, if you love your job, if you love whatever it is that you're passionate about, you're going to talk about it. If you love Jesus, you should talk about it. You should tell the world about Him, you should share that truth. And so there's going to be persecution, there's going to be haters, you have to just stay true to Him and ultimately that's what it's all about."

The critics who wanted Wentz to shut up about his faith and stick to talking about football were about to become some of his biggest fans because the quarterback of their beloved Eagles was about to take them on an incredible journey.

CHAPTER FIVE

MAKING DISCIPLES

The rain started early in the morning on Wednesday, September 6, 2017, and never let up. But this was a special day for students, staff, and faculty at Eastern University and Mother Nature wasn't going to ruin it.

Carson Wentz was coming to campus with teammates Trey Burton and Stefen Wisniewski for a live *Faith On The Field Show* event that had been planned for a couple months.

Rescheduling the event wasn't an option. It was four days before the Philadelphia Eagles played their season opener on the road against the Washington Redskins and the players were generously taking a time-out from their playbook to share the importance of the greatest book of all with students and fans gathered at the suburban Christian school.

NFL players have a hectic schedule during the season. They have practice, meetings, film sessions, workouts, and a game six days a week. They often spend their only day off at the practice facility in the trainer's room or doing extra work to make sure they are mentally and physically prepared. So, postponing an event in the fourth quarter doesn't work for anyone. Wentz, Burton, and Wisniewski sacrificed about five hours out of their day to make an unpaid appearance because they are that passionate about sharing Christ. A little rain or a steady downpour couldn't damper the night.

Crews and volunteers worked tirelessly through the rain to set up the stage, chairs, and video screens and ensure everything was in place for a special evening on the school's soccer field.

Faith and football. It doesn't get any better.

I remember hearing the reaction in the press box when former Eagles receiver Jason Avant would point to heaven after every catch whether he scored a touchdown or gained one yard. One or two writers would mock him, wondering out loud why God cares so much about Avant making a reception. Kurt Warner and Tim Tebow often received the same reaction from certain folks when they praised Jesus. It happens to other Christian athletes too.

I knew Avant's story, a remarkable journey from selling drugs as a twelve-year-old gang member growing up on the South Side of Chicago to disciple for Christ. He wasn't giving thanks because he caught the ball. He was giving God glory for the gift of salvation through Christ.

"When I lift my hands up, it's me saying 'Lord, I know where I could be and I thank You for where I am,'" Avant once told me. "There were times when I was growing up when I didn't have enough to scrounge up a quarter to get an ICEE. I remember the times our house was shot up. I remember when I didn't have any avenues, when I sold drugs. So I lift my hands up and thank the Lord for all He has done for me."

Avant was an integral part of the Christian culture inside the Eagles' locker room that had strong roots. Hall of Famer Reggie White—the Minister of Defense—was a galvanizing force in the late 1980s. Troy Vincent brought discipleship to the team in the late 1990s, early 2000s. He passed the leadership to Brian Dawkins, who gave it to Avant. Nick Foles took the leadership after Avant left and a collection of players—Trey Burton, Jordan Matthews, Chris Maragos, Zach Ertz—stepped up after Foles was traded in 2015.

"Through Troy Vincent's strong leadership, he was really discipling them to manhood through Christ, and that culture created a bond of brothers at that time," Pastor Ted Winsley said.

It bothered me when I heard other writers ridicule Avant, especially because I experienced how a relationship with Christ had transformed me. I understood that players weren't praising God for victory but rather for His grace. I wanted to give them a platform to share their stories. I wrote a couple books in which 104 present and former football and baseball players shared their favorite Bible verses. But I wanted to do more. I love covering Philadelphia sports for The Associated Press, the world's largest news-gathering agency. However, I wanted to find ways to combine my passion for sports and Christ to make a strong impact on people's lives. I was thinking about full-time ministry when I had a conversation with Pastor Kyle Horner in October 2016 that changed my perspective.

"Take Jesus to your marketplace," Horner told me. "They need you there."

Those were powerful words that stuck with me. I believe God gave me certain talents and a platform for a reason so I can spread the gospel.

A few months after that conversation, I created *Faith On The Field Show* with help from cohosts Doug Horton and Pastor Phil Moser. We launched on Philadelphia's 610 ESPN radio on April 6, 2017, with Hall of Famer Mike Schmidt as the first guest. My mission was simple: make disciples. I wanted to use sports as a vehicle to connect people to Jesus by giving athletes a forum to talk about the work our Savior has done in their lives.

Carson Wentz, Trey Burton, and Stefen Wisniewski share my passion for making disciples. We discussed the possibility of offering water baptism to anyone in the crowd who wanted to make a public commitment to Christ at the Eastern event but logistics interfered.

It was incredible to see how God's plan was unfolding, and it was unprecedented to be hosting a sports-themed Christian show on a sports-talk radio station.

More than two thousand people flooded Eastern University's picturesque campus located in beautiful St. David's, Pennsylvania, about forty-five minutes from the team's practice facility in Philadelphia. Tickets were free, and seats were available on a first-come basis so they arrived early and sat for a couple hours in the rain, wearing ponchos that a school official had purchased online earlier in the week when the weather forecast looked ominous.

When a limo bus pulled into the parking lot forty-five minutes before kickoff, students immediately rushed to catch a glimpse of Wentz and his teammates. This was a sports version of a Justin Bieber concert. Wentz, Burton, and Wisniewski are shy, unassuming guys who are uncomfortable with people fussing over them. Still, they graciously posed for pictures and engaged in conversation with everyone who approached.

Then it was show time.

I invited Philadelphia media personality Howard Eskin—who was nicknamed "The King" by baseball legend Pete Rose in the 1980s—to be the special master of ceremony. I grew up listening to Eskin host afternoon drive on 610 WIP-AM and watched him anchoring sports news on television. I was one of his producers when I began my career in radio after college. Eskin, who hosted six thousand radio shows during his career, is the Eagles' sideline reporter on flagship station SportsRadio 94 WIP-FM. He had been peppering me with questions about Christianity. Whenever a tragedy struck such as Hurricane Harvey or the Las Vegas shooting, Eskin would ask me the most difficult question believers try to tackle: "Why does God let bad things happen to good people?"

He also posed this question to Carson Wentz many times. We thought having Eskin on stage to hear the message would help him in his spiritual journey. As he began the introductions, Wentz, Burton, Wisniewski, and Horner circled together behind the stage under an awning. They listened on a cell phone to Elevation Worship's song "Fullness."

Tongues of fire

Testifying of the Son

One desire

Spirit come, Spirit come

They prayed that the Holy Spirit would touch Eskin's heart and lead him to accept Jesus Christ as his Lord and Savior.

It was a private moment, hidden from the spotlight, that revealed so much about their character. On a night when thousands came to see them, these men were most concerned about another man's soul because their goal is to make disciples.

Several months later, I told Eskin about that special moment. He said he's still examining his beliefs but was touched by their personal interest in his salvation.

"I'm blown away by the fact that they would pray for me and have that kind of concern for me," he said. "They're the kind of people who would pray for a lot of people, but the fact it was directed toward me, it really makes me feel good that they care. That night blew me away. It was raining, and to see all those people, I don't think they came out just to see players. They came out for the experience for themselves, and I'm sure it's a great way to see players in another light. I was thoroughly impressed with everyone involved and that the people were into it for the right reason."

Wentz, Burton, and Wisniewski spoke to the crowd for one hour, sharing powerful stories about how God worked in their lives and explaining the brotherhood on the team. Wentz talked about his spiritual growth, his trip to Haiti, the significance of his charity foundation, and his love for his teammates. He also shared his prayer habits, giving a helpful reminder that we don't need to be inside a church building to speak to God.

"With just the nature of our lives, especially during season, we talk about how can we keep growing in our faith, even though we're so busy, but the thing about Jesus is you can go to Him at any time," Wentz said. "Jesus is available at all times, anywhere, and it's a beautiful thing. I'll be driving my thirty-minute drive into the facility, and I'll be in prayer half of that time. And going out to practice, I'll pray as I'm literally doing my warmups, as I'm about to go lift weights, between meetings. It doesn't necessarily have to be this crazy in-depth prayer, but it refocuses your mind, and it's all about living your life in a constant relationship with the Lord. Anytime I have a break, to just ease my mind, even if it's just a twenty-second prayer or twenty-minute prayer, it doesn't matter. Just giving God that attention and being in that constant relationship with Him is a beautiful thing."

Burton talked about the challenges he overcame in college, the night he baptized five teammates in the cold tub, and a mission trip to the Dominican Republic with International Justice Mission. A father of three children, Burton also shared valuable wisdom about being a strong father figure for our kids.

"I grew up without a father, didn't have a man in my life, especially a godly man," he said. "Knowing now I have to have my own relationship with the Lord, there was nobody I could sit there and model my life after, so it was tough, but through God's grace and sitting there with my wife in constant prayer and just trying to include God in every decision we make, He's revealed so much to us on how to be a parent and what godly parents are supposed to look like and what God calls you to do as a parent so it's been really fun, really neat, and I've been completely surrounded with men of God who I enjoy being around."

Wisniewski broke down the misconception that Christians are soft and timid. Football players are tough on the field yet still honor God.

"In the Bible, especially the Old Testament, there are warriors. David was a warrior," he explained. "We fight a different way. God loved David. He loved his heart. He was a passionate warrior. Jesus was the lion and the lamb. We're called to be like Christ and be both. Christ surrendered His life as a lamb but He also was a lion. He's king of the world and He reigns. There's no lion tamer that can handle Christ. We have Him living in us as Christians. On a football field, it's to our advantage because we have the eternal God fighting for us, fighting through us. There's times we're called to be like lambs but there's times we're called to be lions and be fierce and be bold for Christ."

At the end of the program, Eskin had an opportunity to ask his question on stage.

"Why do bad things happen to good people?"

Doug Horton, a professor at Eastern University in addition to cohost of the show, tackled the difficult topic. Horton and his wife, Chris, lost their infant son, Luke, a few years earlier. They relied on their faith to deal with the tragedy. "I don't really think it matters if you are a good person or a bad person," Horton said. "It's not like good people deserve a pass. The issue is this world is full of sin and we are all guilty. We all have a choice of what we want to believe and how we will respond to every situation. I grew up in a Christian home going to church and attending Christian school. I choose to come here to Eastern in part because of its Christian mission. I found that when Luke passed away, I was at a crossroad. Would I forsake everything I had learned and said I believed, or would I cling with everything I have to the promises and character of God? There was no sitting on the fence. I had to choose. Whatever path I chose, I knew I would have to be all in. I chose to trust God's will and plan even though I was completely broken. Trusting God doesn't mean the pain goes away. After three years, it is still raw. What it does is offer a hope for the future and that God will use the tragedy for His glory."

Horner concluded the evening with a strong message on salvation and an invitation to accept Christ.

"The reality is this: the easiest definition of sin is doing something that God is not doing. Sin is active and passive. The wages of sin is death. Just one sin, the legal court of heaven passes judgement that we are guilty of death. So that's the reality of where we are. But if we come to that conclusion, which I hope you can tonight if we're honest with ourselves, there's actually a real hope in it," Horner preached. "The people you see on the stage have come to that conclusion, and when we look at it from that perspective, we see how amazing God's love is for us. Because we'll see that God loves us when we don't deserve anything. The Bible says we're worthy of death . . . But Jesus was willing to take our place on the cross . . . The bad news is that none of us, no matter how hard we try, we'll never be good enough to earn God's love or deserve it. The good news is this: it's not about your goodness, it's about His. God is good and He loves you. And although the wages of sin is death, the gift of God is eternal life through Jesus Christ, a gift you can't earn, but you can receive it.

"So what will you do with the gift God wants to extend to you tonight? Tonight, we want to give you an opportunity to respond to that love of God that we don't deserve. We are sinners in need of a Savior. We can't do it on our own so Jesus made a way for you and me. I know you've been sitting in the rain, and I know you've come to hear the testimonies of these guys. They're not here tonight for just another appearance. They have a thousand other things to do. But they came tonight because the greatest thing in their life is a relationship with the Creator who made them, and they want you to be able to participate in that as well.

"Here's the good news. The Bible says this: if you confess Jesus with your mouth as Lord of your life and believe in your heart that what He did for you on the cross is enough, that God loves you and wants to spend eternity with you, that He's inviting you into a relationship. Notice we didn't say a religion, we didn't say you have to go out and do eighty-eight thousand different things in order to get God on your side; we're simply asking you to realize that God loves you just the way you are and that He wants to have a relationship with you now and forever. So if you confess with your mouth and believe in your heart that Jesus died for you and rose again, the Bible says that tonight you'll be made new.

"Tonight is your night. Doesn't matter what you've done. Doesn't matter how far you've gone away from God, tonight is your night. I'm not saying if you pray this prayer everything will be peachy keen, because the reality is, when you come to Christ, it doesn't mean nothing bad will ever happen to you; but what it means is that it will keep peace in the midst of your tragedy because Jesus will show up there. I can't tell you tragedy won't come but I can tell you that you won't go through it alone, because the King of peace wants to walk you through it.

"Tonight is your night. If you would ask Jesus into your life, your life will forever be different. Tonight is a powerful night. You heard from great men. You heard good stories and sad stories. You heard inspiration and you heard dedication. But tonight the greatest message is this: For God so loved you, that He did everything He had to do and gave His only son. Without you making a deal with Him, He sent Jesus so that you could be forgiven and you get to know Him intimately day by day.

"So I want to pray with you because the Bible says there's power when people pray together. There's thousands of people here because Jesus is here. You're not praying to me, you're praying to the Lord of Lords. If you want to pray with me, just raise your hands. Let's stand and we're gonna all pray . . . Dear Lord

Jesus, Here I am today. I've come to give You my life. All that I am, all that I have, all that I ever will be, I give to You now. I'm asking You, Jesus, to be the Lord and Savior of my life. Forgive me of all my sins, cleanse me of everything I've done wrong, fill me with Your Spirit and make me Your child from this day forward and forever more, I choose to live full on for Jesus Christ. I won't go back and I won't look back because I know now the best of my life is yet to come. In Jesus's name, Amen."

Many hands went up and people prayed for salvation as rain continued to fall on their heads, a sort of water baptism without the pool. A young man who turned to the Lord that night told one of the volunteers handing out Bibles, "I came here to see Carson Wentz and the Eagles. I got something more important than that."

He was just one of many disciples made that night.

CHAPTER

SIX

IRON SHARPENS IRON

One day after the Philadelphia Eagles lost to the Green Bay Packers in their 2017 preseason opener, the reality that the NFL is a cruel business hit Carson Wentz hard. Jordan Matthews was traded to the Buffalo Bills along with a 2018 third-round draft pick for cornerback Ronald Darby. Wentz and Matthews had just traveled to Haiti together a few months earlier. Matthews was his go-to wide receiver on the field and one of his closest buddies off the field. Everyone on the team loved Matthews, a hard worker who did whatever he could to help his teammates. Wentz, Matthews, Trey Burton, Zach Ertz, Jordan Hicks, and Chris Maragos were the core of the team's Christian brotherhood. Proverbs 27:17 says: "As iron sharpens iron, so one person sharpens another." These men truly sharpened each other. They lifted each other when someone was down. They encouraged each other in tough times and pushed each other to dig deeper in their relationship with the Lord. The six players gathered for an emotional sendoff dinner the night the trade went down, and then drove Matthews to the airport.

"It's tough. This is my first time experiencing this with someone that's one of my best friends," Wentz said a day later. "It's tough on him too. It's kind of out of the blue. Replacing a guy like that in the locker room is not going to be easy."

Pastor Ted Winsley reminded the players the trade would give Matthews an opportunity to impact a new set of teammates.

"Whenever someone leaves, it is because you have an assignment and you are supposed to take it and share it," Winsley said. "This was a reminder how precious it is, and it was a reminder of why we're together, to become rooted, to become grounded, and then to spread it. Players, when they leave Philadelphia, they tell other players that what we have here is special."

Christianity is nothing new to the NFL. Many players from Reggie White to Kurt Warner to Tim Tebow have boldly professed their faith. The 2012 Super Bowl champion Baltimore Ravens had a strong Christian contingent led by Ray Lewis. Same for the 2013 champion Seattle Seahawks with Russell Wilson. But the 2017 Eagles were a different breed of young players who passionately shared the gospel, held each other accountable, and encouraged, motivated, and inspired each other to walk their talk daily.

"We had a great brotherhood in Seattle, guys who loved Jesus passionately and were committed to the Lord, and that was the cool thing because you saw guys who were willing to put that much more into their sport because they knew they were honoring the Lord through their gifts and talents and abilities, so you saw the sacrifices probably even greater because they knew they were playing for something greater, and the same here with the Eagles," said Maragos, who played for the Seahawks from 2011–13. "We want to bring the Lord as much glory as possible."

Torrey Smith, who was part of Baltimore's championship team and spent two seasons with the San Francisco 49ers before coming to Philadelphia, was impressed by the young leaders on the Eagles.

"I think here the difference is a lot of younger guys lead," Smith said. "As men, you tend to be very sheltered. If I am going through some things, I may not express that to the next man. Only you can expose your weaknesses and the things you want to work on, whether it's in your relationship or your marriage or your family. When you're able to talk about it among your brothers, among your family, it helps you grow. And when you realize that you can apply biblical principles to it, it helps us all grow."

Stefen Wisniewski also played for other teams before joining the Eagles. He began his career with the Oakland Raiders and spent one year with the Jacksonville Jaguars before coming to Philadelphia in 2016.

"Obviously, there have been Christians before," he said. "It's just so special that there are so many on one team and so many that I would call committed or mature, who are believers, who are solid in their faith, and so many who are outspoken about their faith. There's a lot of guys who would prefer to keep their faith private for whatever reason, and I think most of the Christians on this team have embraced the fact that we have a platform to share Christ. It's a huge platform. Millions of people follow us. Let's use it to lift high the name of Jesus. It's so cool that so many guys have embraced that, and the fact that the quarterback is one of them, both quarterbacks, I think helps because that's the most visible position."

Before the Eagles drafted him, Wentz prayed daily that he would go to a team and be surrounded by guys who helped him grow closer in his relationship to Christ. He could not have imagined a better situation.

"Honestly, it's been the most incredible thing being here with these guys in our locker room," Wentz said. "I think a lot of people miss out, I know I did early in college to some extent, in understanding the true value of community, the true value of what we talked about—iron sharpening iron or spurring each other on. God Himself is God the Father, the Son, the Holy Spirit—three in one. He Himself is living in a relationship in a community. When Jesus sent out the disciples, He sent them out two by two because they need each other to spur each other on. And I think that we can all lose sight of that and say, 'Well I've got my faith and you have yours, or I have this and you do your own thing.' And that's not what it's all about, because life is hard. Life is messy. There are a lot of things that just aren't good in life, and it's easy to just get lost and wander. You always just need people to help keep you on the straight and narrow—keep you on that path and really encourage you. I just know how really beneficial it's been in my life to have brothers in Christ and to really just help keep me on that path, and I really encourage [people] to kind of just check yourself to some extent and see who's in your life. Are they building you up? Are they lifting you up? Are they spurring you on? Are they tearing you down? There's value in iron sharpening iron."

Accountability is an important part of the team's brotherhood. Often those who walk closely with the Lord are going to be challenged by the enemy and pulled in the wrong direction, so having accountability partners is a vital part of the Christian journey. Being an accountability partner can be a tough job because sometimes it requires calling someone out—this should be done privately—and it could risk alienating a friend who doesn't want to hear the truth. But several of the players on the Eagles had the courage to hold each other accountable, and equally important, they were willing to be held accountable. One player told me one of his teammates pulled him aside after he reacted angrily to questions from reporters and gently reminded him that it was important to represent Christ at all times. He thought twice about lashing out the next time he faced difficult questions.

"Even when we are not at Bible study, it is a fellowship," Ertz said. "Those guys are holding me accountable. Off the field, I am holding them accountable as well. We truly care about each other, we truly care about the growth that each individual has in the Word, as believers, as well as friends and family. There are a lot of guys who are truly trying to boost me up along the way and keep me focused on the main thing, which is obviously the Word and Jesus.

"We probably have seven guys that we were really vulnerable with. When I go back to California sometimes in the offseason, the hardest part is being away from these guys because I don't have someone walking the walk like I am so much as I do back in Philadelphia. If I am slipping up, Jordan [Hicks] is going to be there for me and say, 'Zach, we need to talk about this,' and the same thing with Jordan. We are able to be vulnerable because everything Jordan has gone through I've gone through at times; just that ability to hold each other accountable to something so much bigger than us."

That strong desire to grow in their faith, to sharpen each other, to hold each other accountable helped this core group of players form an unbreakable bond.

"We wouldn't be who we are, we wouldn't be the men in Christ that we are without each other," Hicks said. "I think community is such a powerful concept that Christ has given us and we are just so blessed to have. I look back on my past, and it is a miracle that I am with the Philadelphia Eagles. I've had so any different injuries, and there are so many different ways I could have fallen off, but the fact that we have such a community that we can bounce ideas off each other. We can dive deep; it is such a huge thing because being vulnerable with someone, you know they know everything, and it is a scary place to be. But when you go there, that is when the real change happens. You can hit those points that hurt. We're lucky and blessed to be in the situation that we are and know that not everyone is in a locker room where they can have that type of access to each other every single day. We see each other every day all the time, and we are lucky to have that. Community is such a strong concept that you know I think that every believer should have."

Losing Jordan Matthews meant Carson Wentz was entering the season throwing to only one wide receiver he played with during his rookie year. The Eagles revamped the position in the offseason to give Wentz more weapons. They signed Alshon Jeffery and Torrey Smith in free agency and drafted rookies Mack Hollins and Shelton Gibson. Only Nelson Agholor was back from 2016 and he showed plenty of improvement in training camp after going through major struggles that led to his benching the previous season.

Fittingly, Agholor teamed with Wentz to deliver a highlight-reel play that kicked off the 2017 regular season in style. On the team's first offensive series in the first game at Washington, Wentz put all his spectacular skills on display on one play. He dropped back to throw and felt pressure, so he spun away from a tackler. He started to run and eluded another tackler and then stopped. He saw Agholor was wide open downfield. Wentz was off-balance, but he fired the ball deep. Agholor jumped to make the catch, broke a tackle, and scored a 58-yard touchdown. It was a preview of many exciting plays yet to come. The Eagles beat the Redskins 30–17. Everyone was talking about Wentz's Houdini escape after the game.

"That's just what he does, man. He's special. He's dynamic," Eagles right tackle Lane Johnson said about his quarterback. "He can make great plays with his feet. Sometimes, it looks like a sack is coming, and he can get out under it and make plays. He's a special player."

The Eagles went to Kansas City the following week to play the Chiefs and their former coach, Andy Reid. But Alex Smith and Kareem Hunt followed up sensational performances in a victory over the Patriots in Week 1 with another strong effort against Philadelphia. The Eagles couldn't give Doug Pederson a win over his mentor. They lost 27–20 to the Chiefs. It would be the last time the Eagles tasted defeat for nearly three months.

Just like they sharpened each other off the field, they did so on the field too. They watched film, identified mistakes that led to the loss and corrected them, setting up a long winning streak ahead.

CHAPTER SEVEN

A FIRM FOUNDATION

Carson Wentz stood on the sideline anxiously awaiting Jake Elliott's 61-yard field-goal attempt with the score tied at 24–24 and only a few seconds remaining in a Week 3 game against the New York Giants.

The Eagles and Giants—division rivals separated by ninety-six miles along I-95—went back and forth for more than fifty-nine minutes on a humid Sunday afternoon in late September. It was early in the season, but the Giants had already lost their first two and going 0–3 would be difficult to overcome for a team many considered a strong contender—I picked them to win the NFC East. The Eagles couldn't afford to lose their home opener to a division opponent if they wanted to be a serious challenger.

Now, the game would come down to a rookie kicker who had joined the team only twelve days earlier.

Elliott signed with the Eagles after Caleb Sturgis was injured in Week 1 against Washington. He was on Cincinnati's practice squad when Philly called. Elliott had already missed two field goals and one extra point in his first two games. Making a 61-yard try seemed unlikely. No rookie had ever done it and only eleven kickers in league history had ever made a field goal from that distance or longer.

Wentz had fired a perfect 19-yard sideline pass to Alshon Jeffery to set up the attempt. He went to the sideline while the field-goal unit ran on the field. Wentz was pacing, nervously anticipating the kick.

"This guy is a superhero if he makes it. I'll give him my game check if he makes it," Wentz shouted.

That's no small change. Wentz earned $31,764.71 per game during the 2017 season.

Kamu Grugier-Hill replied: "He made it one time in practice."

Unfazed, Wentz repeated, "I'll give him my game check if he makes it."

Wentz took a knee next to Jeffery and Torrey Smith while Hill bent over and put his hands on his knees. The snap was on target and the hold was perfect. Elliott approached the ball and drilled it with his right foot, sending it between the uprights and just over the crossbar to give the Eagles a 27–24 victory.

Wentz screamed: "Whoooooooooooooooooo!" He ran onto the field with the rest of the team, and they mobbed Elliott. Hill and Mychal Kendricks carried him off the field.

Welcome to Philly, kid.

The video of Wentz promising to give Elliott his game check went viral, and he proved to be a man of his word. Elliott didn't accept Wentz's game check but agreed on a donation to a charity of his choice instead.

"It was funny," Wentz said. "Obviously, it blew up a lot more than we thought it would. It was really cool how we captured that whole moment. You don't see 61-yard game-winners very often, and I just happened to be mic'd up and saying some random things, but it was all funny. I talked to Jake afterward, and I kind of wanted to donate some of it to a charity of his choice, so that's what we're going to do."

Wentz, of course, had no regrets about giving up the money. "I never lose sleep over helping others."

That successful 61-yard field goal kicked off quite a run for the Eagles.

A week later, another newcomer was the hero. Running back LeGarrette Blount had 136 yards rushing in a 26–24 win on the road against the Los Angeles Chargers. Blount was part of two Super Bowl championship teams in New England and led the NFL with eighteen rushing touchdowns a season earlier but remained unsigned as a free agent for two months before the Eagles gave him a one-year contract. He brought a winning attitude and veteran presence to the offense. His bruising running style was on full display when he powered through the Chargers' defense for a 68-yard scamper that fired up his teammates.

"I know I'm one of the better backs in this league as far as running the football," Blount said. "I'm always going to run with that passion and with that confidence."

The Eagles improved to 4–1 by dominating the Arizona Cardinals 34–7 in Week 5. Wentz tossed three touchdown passes on three consecutive attempts in the first quarter, including a 59-yard bomb to Smith. The score led to one of the best celebrations of the season. The NFL finally relaxed its rules on touchdown celebrations, allowing players to get creative. The Eagles had fun with this throughout the season, coming up with some innovative routines.

Smith and his buddies had an original idea for a baseball-themed celebration. After kneeling down to say a prayer, Smith stood up in the end zone and pretended to be a batter. Jeffery crouched down behind him like a catcher. Nelson Agholor was the pitcher. Wentz was the umpire behind Jeffery. Agholor went through a wind-up and tossed an imaginary pitch. Smith, holding the football as if it was a bat, took a mighty swing at the fake baseball and hit a home run.

"That prayer meant a whole lot," Smith said. "When you are going through things, to stay level headed, don't get too high or too low, that is how I live my life in every situation. For us to have a good week of practice and stay focused, and I had the opportunity to make it count, especially being here at home, it meant a lot."

The team was winning, players were having fun, and everybody was part of it.

Being inclusive was important to the core group of Christians on the Eagles. They didn't want to alienate any teammates and made sure to let them know all were welcome regardless of their beliefs. Some locker rooms in the NFL and in other sports are divided. Players socialize in groups whether it's offensive players hanging out with other offensive players or guys separating into positions. But camaraderie was important to the Eagles and spreading the love of Christ should never be exclusive.

"You never want to be labeled as a clique in anything, especially in Jesus, because now you're separated from everybody," Carson Wentz said. "You always want to be open. The number one thing is we always try to be accountable to each other and to how we love and honor everybody on the team and how we show them the love of Christ in our actions. People know what we're about because we post on social media and talk about Jesus, but the people around us every single day see how we're acting and how we walk the walk, how we treat them, how we treat the people in the cafeteria, how we treat our coaches, how we approach our job."

On several occasions, I saw Wentz and other players sacrifice their time signing countless autographs for fans on hot days during training camp, going out of their way to pose for pictures and selfies, and generally being nice to everyone they encountered. They were always respectful, humble, sincere.

"It's not always what you say, but people are led to Christ by your actions, how you live," Wentz continued. "So we always keep the door open, we love on people and never judge them because they have a different view or background, and we just keeping praying because God ultimately is the one who changes hearts. We can just plant the seeds."

Wentz was touched by the outpouring of brotherhood he encountered from the minute he walked into Philadelphia's locker room. Trey Burton approached him to chat about his faith after noticing Wentz's tattoos. There's *AO1* on his right wrist and a large cross between his shoulder blades with *Isaiah 41:10* written above it. The Bible verse says, "So do not fear, for I am with you; do not be dismayed, for I am your God. I will strengthen you and help you; I will uphold you with my righteous right hand."

Burton, Chris Maragos, and Jordan Matthews invited Wentz to go with them to Pastor Kyle Horner's church. Horner is a passionate preacher who has a knack for making you want to become a better person in every area of your life simply through conversation.

"When I walked in day one, they're inviting me to church, inviting me to Bible studies, and it's been unbelievable seeing God's faithfulness answering that prayer for me," Wentz said, referring to when he asked God before the draft to lead him to a team of believers. "And, it's not just players but coaches too. It's just the culture in that organization and the love for Christ runs deep in that building.

"We were created to live in community, to have those relationships, to not walk alone because life is hard, stuff comes up for everybody, myself included, and without those brothers in Christ and those people in your life in your corner, I don't know where I'd be. I praise God and thank God for His constant faithfulness and putting the right people in my life at the right time and surrounding me with so many people. As far as work goes, going in each day knowing there's a bunch of brothers in Christ and believers around me, it changes the culture, it changes how we act and how we do life, and it really translates on the field. I can look at Zach Ertz after I make a bad throw, and we still love each other. It's a different dynamic when you have Jesus as the common denominator. It changes everything."

Ertz recalled a conversation with Jason Avant during his rookie season in 2013. Avant was the spiritual leader on the team playing his eighth and final season with the Eagles. Ertz, an All-American at Stanford University, was still growing in his faith.

"Jason is a guy that radiates the gospel," Ertz said. "He was a guy that was always welcoming to me. I would sit next to him in all the special-teams meetings. I remember one day we were watching film and something happened on the field and I said: 'Jesus Christ.' I said that in vain. Before I really dedicated my life, I didn't know the profound impact of what I was saying. And Jason goes,

'Jesus doesn't have anything to do with that play.' So that's something I still remember to this day. The guy was so welcoming to me. He is a phenomenal person, and he definitely opened the door. All you have to do with people is open the door. It's not our job to bang it; we just have to open the door, and God will do the rest.

"The characteristic that we want to portray is love. We are not coming into any situation with any given advantage. We want to show the praise and love for Jesus that He shows us every day. There are guys in the locker room that aren't believers, but we love them regardless."

Players are careful not to push their faith on teammates. They are respectful of each guy's situation and recognize some aren't ready to commit to Christ, and certain players might never be open to it.

"We've had conversation about this, and it's just living life with these guys," Jordan Hicks said. "They are going through issues that we walked through. Whatever these guys are going through, it's not going to last. It's a matter of showing love in a sincere way. There's a difference from trying to push somebody into your belief and just trying to express and show your love. You want to help, that's what you really want to do."

Howie Roseman credited Doug Pederson for creating an environment in which the players strive to be inclusive.

"The NFL really is the ultimate melting pot, bringing together players and coaches from all different backgrounds, cultures, and religions," Roseman said. "It's a testament to Coach Pederson and his staff that our players feel comfortable expressing their beliefs in a respectful way. When people are able to express themselves freely, that helps build trust, which is the foundation of any strong team."

CHAPTER EIGHT

FAITH WITHOUT WORKS IS DEAD

Chris Long knew he had to do something after seeing the violent protests through the streets of the University of Virginia's quaint campus in Charlottesville on August 11–12, 2017. An ugly scene unfolded during a rally to protest the removal of a nearby Robert E. Lee statue. White supremacy groups clashed with counterprotestors. A woman was killed and dozens were injured. It was horrible.

Long, who went to high school and college in Charlottesville, couldn't stand to see the civil unrest in his hometown. He was appalled not because of where it happened, but because it took place anywhere in this country. Of course it was especially difficult to see it happen so close to home.

"It was really hard to watch," Long said. "But that's the ugly stuff that affects a lot of people on a daily basis. It's a sad reality."

Long joined the Eagles as a free agent in March after he won a Super Bowl in his only season with the Patriots. He spent the first eight years of his NFL career playing for the St. Louis Rams and brought strong leadership to Philadelphia's locker room.

The tragedy in Charlottesville inspired Long to show his support for players who were using demonstrations during the national anthem as a way to protest against social injustices. Colin Kaepernick began the movement in 2016 by taking a knee during "The Star Spangled Banner." The stance cost the former San Francisco 49ers quarterback a job because he was not in the NFL a year later.

Long, who is white, decided to put his arm around Malcolm Jenkins, who is black, while his teammate stood on the sideline with a fist raised during the anthem. The sign of unity that Long displayed for the first time at a preseason game days after the violence in his hometown brought him more attention than anything he'd ever done on the field.

"It's a good time for people who look like me to be here for people fighting for equality," Long said. "If you don't see why you need allies for people that are fighting for equality right now, I don't think you'll ever see it. Malcolm is a leader, and I'm here to show support as a white athlete."

Jenkins appreciated the gesture.

"I think he understands that he could never necessarily know my experience as a black male, but in light of all that's going on, as a white male, he understands that he needs to be an ally," Jenkins said.

Long later announced that he was donating his first six game checks to fund scholarships in Charlottesville. Then he decided to give his last ten game checks to help launch an initiative to increase educational opportunities in the three cities where he played: St. Louis, Boston, and Philadelphia. His contribution totaled a million dollars.

"Educational opportunity and equity are the best gateway to a better tomorrow for everyone in America," Long said. "We want to promote diversity and equality and educational opportunity. That's something I've been passionate about for a couple of years. I'm not the only person to donate money to charities. But my platform allows me an opportunity to inspire people to do the same."

Long grew up around football. His dad, Howie Long, is a Hall of Fame defensive lineman who played thirteen seasons for the Raiders. He wasn't a kid whose parents struggled to put food on the table. Having a lot didn't stop Chris Long from trying to relate to and help those who have little.

"There's a need for equality across racial lines and also equality between rich and poor," Long said.

Long, who isn't outspoken about his faith, and Jenkins, a strong Christian, became partners for social activism, trying to promote racial equality and reform in the education, criminal justice, and law enforcement systems. They were among a small group of players who invited Eagles owner Jeffrey Lurie and NFL commissioner Roger Goodell to meet with police, grassroots organizations, policy leaders, and public defenders in Philadelphia. That meeting took place after the first game of the season. Long and Jenkins donated their time and money throughout the season to raise awareness for important issues and improve communities. Their outspoken leadership set an excellent example for younger players to strive to make a positive difference off the field.

"I think that's our responsibility," Long said. "Malcolm is an awesome humanitarian and a leader of men. I hope that I am too. We are given so much, so it's the least we can do. This city has been awesome, especially since I was a new guy. They have kind of adopted me. Everything I've done off the field they were a part of and really stepped up. You feel that real bond with the city, and at the end of the day this is the least we can do. Everyone always says to focus on football and be in your playbook, but I think Malcolm and others have proved that you can do positive things in the community and still be successful. The way Malcolm attacks things off the field is the same as how he plays. We're just really lucky to be in this platform."

Said Jenkins, "It's important for professional athletes to use their platform for more than themselves, more than the monetary gains, but to really make an impact."

Jenkins helped to form the Players Coalition, a group of players who work together throughout the country to improve social justice issues focusing on criminal-justice reform, police and community relations, and education and economic advancement in low-income communities and communities of color. The Coalition's negotiations with NFL owners led them to make significant financial contributions to the players' social and political issues. Jenkins eventually stopped raising his fist during the anthem after the owners committed to donating $89 million.

The anthem protest was a divisive issue throughout the season. It even divided Christians because some viewed it as a protest against the anthem itself, or the American flag, or the military, or police.

Jenkins was frustrated by fellow Christians who didn't understand the real purpose behind the demonstrations.

"Countless times in the Bible it talks about fighting for the fatherless, the widows, those who are incarcerated," Jenkins said. "For us to be as blessed as we are, to have the resources, the influence, we feel like that's part of our purpose and because we can, it's almost our responsibility. It's one of those things that usually when you're doing the right thing, you get criticized for. So we understand there's going to be pushback that comes along with it, but if you talk to most of the guys who are doing it, all we ask for is empathy, we ask for understanding, and those things are the core values of being a Christian.

"I feel like the Christian community, as big as we are, as much influence as we have on policy and politics, if the Church ever got behind really being for equality and really being for justice, it would show up, it would come. But a lot of times we don't show the empathy, we don't take the time to listen, and we're just as segregated as the world is right now. There's a lot that the church can be doing to effectuate positive change in this country. We all just have to do our part."

The Eagles avoided those conflicts because they have a strong foundation rooted in faith, mutual respect, and understanding of each other's differences. They found a way to remain unified despite so much tension in the world around them.

"I don't think it matters if you are white or black, we just want to show that love each and every day," Zach Ertz said.

The Eagles had a quick turnaround in Week 6, traveling to Carolina to play the Panthers in a Thursday night game in front of a national television audience.

This would be a marquee matchup. Both teams were 4–1. Carson Wentz vs. Cam Newton. Two strong defenses. A potential playoff preview. A victory for the Eagles would solidify their status as one of the best teams in the conference.

There was no better way to prepare for a big game like this

than to gather the night before at the team hotel for another pool baptism. Marcus Johnson, a second-year pro who caught his first pass in the NFL just a few days earlier in Philadelphia's win against Arizona, wanted to publicly profess his commitment to Christ through water baptism.

After the team finished final meetings and the last walk-through practice before the game, several players gathered around the pool to support Johnson. It was ten o'clock on the night before an important game, but there was nowhere else these brothers in Christ would rather be. Pastor Kyle Horner stood in the pool with Johnson and talked about the symbolism of baptism.

"Paul says baptism is an outward symbol of what happens in our hearts when we come to Jesus," Horner said. "The Bible says when we go under the water it's like entering into His death. When we come up out of the water, we're entering into His resurrected life."

When Johnson emerged from the water, his dreadlocked hair dripping wet, his teammates cheered like he had scored the game-winning touchdown. After Johnson posted a picture of his baptism on social media, it went viral.

Johnson's tweet read: "First time being Baptized! Corporate Worship is a beautiful thing!! Cleansed & Reborn in JESUS name!!"

"It didn't matter where we did it. I wanted to go ahead and take that next step and be baptized," Johnson said. "It's been a true blessing. Being baptized is something you can't do alone. I had been talking to Pastor Kyle about it for a while. God had it meant to be right before that game.

"Since I got to Philly, I've grown in my faith. The people who helped push me in the locker room helped me grow and I'm so thankful that something like a baptism could be so wide-reaching.

So many people reached out to me to say I inspired them. It's a beautiful thing. I didn't think it would blow up the way it did. It's such a blessing."

The anthem protests had dominated the NFL headlines, especially after President Donald Trump criticized players who were taking a knee. But when people talked about the Eagles, it was their faith that stood out.

"I love the fact that these guys are not afraid to put it out there," Horner said a few days after performing the baptism. "It's rewriting some of the narrative of the NFL in light of everything. Every time they talk about the run the Eagles are on, they talk about the faith of these guys, the unity of this team."

The anthem controversy was still the hot topic, but the Eagles and their strong faith provided a much-needed diversion for those who wanted to discuss something else.

On the field, Wentz tossed three touchdown passes, including two to Zach Ertz, to lead the Eagles to a 28–23 victory over the Panthers. They improved to 5–1 and had the best record in the NFC. But their biggest win during the trip to North Carolina was Johnson's baptism.

CHAPTER NINE

THANKFUL THROUGH THE STORM

Chris Maragos is always smiling. He walks through the locker room with a sense of peace that comes from a relationship with Christ. On the field, he's a different animal. Maragos is a hard-hitting safety and standout on special teams for the Eagles. He's known for his ferocious hits and bringing the energy.

So when Maragos suffered a torn knee ligament in the fourth quarter of Philadelphia's win against Carolina on October 12, it felt like a gut-punch to his teammates. He was such an integral part of the team's success and is a tremendous leader and mentor. Maragos got the call from the doctor confirming the severity of his injury fifteen minutes before he received news his wife was going into labor. He didn't have time to sulk. Cambria Rose, the couple's third child, was on her way.

Maragos became the third key player to sustain a season-ending injury in the first six weeks of the 2017 season. Kicker Caleb Sturgis injured his hip in the first game. Darren Sproles, the versatile veteran running back and one of the best punt returners in NFL history, tore a knee ligament and broke his forearm on the same play in the team's win against the Giants in Week 3.

Injuries are challenging, especially when the team is having a great season. Maragos found comfort in his faith.

"You pour your whole life's work to be an NFL player and to get to these moments and then to have an injury that would set you back like this, it's definitely disheartening, but I do have a lot of encouragement, and I do have a lot of confidence knowing that I'm right where I need to be," Maragos said. "The [Bible] says to consider difficult circumstances pure joy because we know that in those difficult times [God] is creating something in me that will make me better and stronger and make me complete as a Christian, as a man, as a member of our community, as a member of our house. So I have to trust."

Maragos was referencing James 1:2–4. It says, "Consider it pure joy, my brothers and sisters, whenever you face trials of many kinds, because you know that the testing of your faith produces perseverance. Let perseverance finish its work so that you may be mature and complete, not lacking anything."

Maragos kept the right perspective through the tough ordeal. He stayed around the team and remained a leader, even though he was on crutches and couldn't run out there and make tackles with reckless abandon. He mentored younger players, encouraged other injured players, and spread positivity.

"God is so gracious that he gives us so many things to get through the difficulties," Maragos said. "Most importantly, he gives

Team chaplain Pastor Ted Winsley (left) baptizes Philadelphia Eagles quarterback Nick Foles and his wife Tori in a pool at The Grand Golf Club in San Diego on March 6, 2015.

Philadelphia Eagles tight end Trey Burton (left) and team chaplain Pastor Ted Winsley (right) baptize former Eagles player David Watford in a cold tub at the team's practice facility in October 2016.

Philadelphia Eagles tight end Trey Burton (left) and team chaplain Pastor Ted Winsley (right) baptize Eagles linebacker Jordan Hicks in a cold tub at the team's practice facility in October 2016.

Ted Winsley

AO1 Foundation

Philadelphia Eagles quarterback Carson Wentz presents a service dog as part of a program through his AO1 Foundation.

Cleats worn by Philadelphia Eagles quarterback Carson Wentz during the NFL's "My Cause, My Cleats" campaign in 2017.

Philadelphia Eagles tight end Zach Ertz (center), linebacker Jordan Hicks (right), and Rob Maaddi (left) pray during a *Faith On The Field Show* event on April 18, 2017.

(From left) Pastor Kyle Horner, Doug Horton, and Rob Maaddi share a laugh with Philadelphia Eagles quarterback Carson Wentz, tight end Trey Burton, and left guard Stefen Wisniewski at a *Faith On The Field Show* event on Sept. 6, 2017.

A large crowd sits for hours in the rain during a live *Faith On The Field Show* event featuring Philadelphia Eagles quarterback Carson Wentz, tight end Trey Burton, and left guard Stefen Wisniewski at Eastern University on Sept. 6, 2017.

Philadelphia Eagles tight end Trey Burton (back row, left), quarterback Carson Wentz (center), and left guard Stefen Wisniewski (right) pose with a group of kids at a *Faith On The Field Show* event on Sept. 6, 2017.

Philadelphia Eagles quarterback Nick Foles poses with superfan Shaun Young.

Seattle Seahawks and Philadelphia Eagles players huddle on bended knee to pray after a game in Seattle, December 2017.

Defensive tackle Fletcher Cox wears a wrestling mask as he takes part in a media event for the NFL Super Bowl 52 football game.

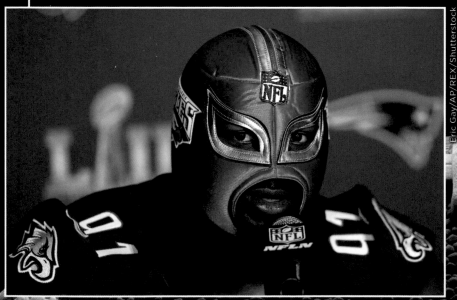

Trey Burton, left, throws a touchdown pass to Nick Foles during the first half of the NFL Super Bowl 52 football game against the New England Patriots.

Quarterback Nick Foles (9) makes a catch for a touchdown.

Tight end Zach Ertz (86) dives for a touchdown past New England Patriots safety Devin McCourty (32) in the third quarter of the Super Bowl.

Foles celebrates a touchdown pass to Zach Ertz during the second half of the Super Bowl.

New England Patriots tight end Rob Gronkowski (87) together with Philadelphia Eagles free safety Rodney McLeod (23) and cornerback Jaylen Watkins (26) jump for a pass in the end zone for the final play of the game.

Nick Foles holds up the Vince Lombardi Trophy after the Super Bowl.

Philadelphia Eagles center Jason Kelce speaks in front of the Philadelphia Museum of Art during a Super Bowl victory event.

Fans cheer as a bus with team members arrives near the Philadelphia Museum of Art during the Super Bowl victory parade.

The Philadelphia Eagles parade up the Benjamin Franklin Parkway toward the Philadelphia Museum of Art during the Super Bowl victory parade in Philadelphia.

Philadelphia Eagles fans celebrate on a garbage truck outside of City Hall after the parade.

Quarterbacks Nick Foles (left), Nate Sudfeld, and Carson Wentz celebrate during the Super Bowl victory parade.

A group of volunteers in Haiti included Pastor Ted Winsley, Eagles receiver Rashard Davis, Pastor Kyle Horner, Eagles tight end Zach Ertz, Eagles quarterback Carson Wentz, and his brother Zach Wentz.

Philadelphia Eagles quarterbacks Nate Sudfeld (left) and Carson Wentz (back) during a mission trip to Haiti in April 2018.

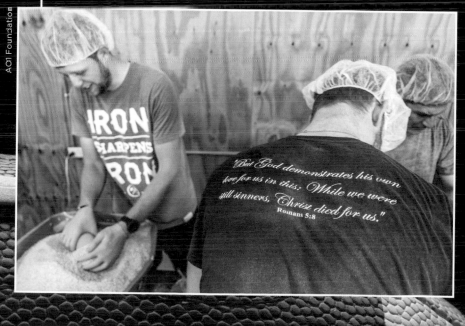

(From right) Philadelphia Eagles quarterback Carson Wentz, *Faith On The Field Show* host Rob Maaddi, and cohosts Doug Horton and Pastor Kyle Horner at an event on April 30, 2018.

Philadelphia Eagles quarterback Carson Wentz (left) is interviewed by Rob Maaddi before the AO1 Foundation inaugural softball game on June 1, 2018.

Philadelphia Eagles quarterback Carson Wentz (standing) chats with teammates Nick Foles and Brandon Brooks (both seated) at the AO1 Foundation inaugural softball game on June 1, 2018.

J. Alan Paul Photography, www.jalanpaul.com

Several Philadelphia Eagles players on the field for a home run derby ahead of Carson Wentz's AO1 Foundation inaugural softball game on June 1, 2018.

J. Alan Paul Photography, www.jalanpaul.com

us His Word, which guides us and gives us the truth and the substance of our being and gives us our guiding lamp in terms of how we're trying to navigate through life. What I've been super grateful for from a personal level, He gives us great relationships with solid believers and other people who are fighting the fight and walking this walk on a daily basis. We have such a great group of guys who have been supporting me, showing love, praying for me, staying in touch, and hanging out."

Little did Maragos know he soon would have more company in the trainer's room.

The Eagles had ten days off between a pair of prime-time games in October. After beating the Panthers on the road, they returned home for a Monday-night matchup against the Washington Redskins.

I started that day in New York doing a one-hour video interview with Pastor Carl Lentz, the charismatic preacher who helped grow Australia-based Hillsong into a multi-location megachurch in the U.S. Lentz, a huge sports fan and former college basketball player, is known for pastoring Justin Bieber and NBA stars Kyrie Irving and Kevin Durant, but he treats everyone in his congregation like an all-star. Of the thousands of interviews I've done in my career, this was my favorite because I have tremendous respect for Lentz and share his passion to spread the gospel to everyone whether it's a superstar athlete or a homeless guy on the street. But the ride back to Philly was super long because New York city traffic was congested, as usual. I arrived at Lincoln Financial Field about a half-hour before kickoff. I was so late that I got a chance to see something I had never seen in my life. Outside the stadium, people were holding signs that read: "Seek Jesus, Not a Church" and "God Created You Unique and Intelligent. Find Your Purpose in Jesus." I had been to hundreds of games first as a fan and then as a reporter but never before saw believers carrying signs like these near an NFL stadium. I truly believed Carson Wentz's boldness had empowered these Christians to speak out. I asked a long-time Philadelphia writer about it, and he agreed that it was Wentz's influence.

Wentz and the offense started the game off slowly but took control after the Redskins jumped to a 10–3 lead. Wentz fired three touchdown passes in a span of nine minutes between the second and third quarters. He tossed another touchdown to a fourth different receiver in the fourth quarter and the Eagles won 34–24.

Afterward, I told Wentz in the locker room about my visit with Lentz, and he said he was hoping to see him preach at Hillsong. I also showed him the pictures I took of the people carrying the Jesus signs before the game. He's too humble to take credit for influencing them.

But the night was costly for the Eagles.

Jason Peters, the nine-time Pro Bowl left tackle who protected Wentz's blind side, suffered a torn right knee ligament in the third quarter. Everyone had so much respect for Peters that the entire team walked onto the field while he was sitting on a golf cart and one player after another shook his hand, tapped his shoulder, or offered an encouraging word.

Fans chanted his name, but Peters was most concerned about giving his replacement, second-year pro Halapoulivaati Vaitai, some advice. Peters pulled Big V close and told him, "Just keep your composure and calm down."

Peters is a quiet leader, someone who leads more by example

than words. He stays away from the spotlight and doesn't talk much to the media. His teammates appreciate his work ethic and team-first attitude.

"He is a legend around here. He is a future Hall of Famer. We love that guy. He means a lot to us," Wentz said.

The Eagles suffered a double whammy in that game.

Jordan Hicks, the playmaking quarterback of the defense, went down on the second play of the game. He was carried off the field and taken to the sideline where Maragos consoled him while he waited for a cart to take him to the locker room. It was initially called an ankle injury, but it turned out Hicks had ruptured his right Achilles tendon and also was going to miss the rest of the season.

Sturgis. Sproles. Maragos. Now Peters and Hicks. The Eagles had adopted "We all we got, we all we need" as their rallying cry earlier in the season as an inspirational way of reminding each other it didn't matter what the outside world thought of them, they were family and believed in each other. Malcolm Jenkins would finish a pep talk with "1–2–3" and players would respond, "We all we got." Jenkins would then say: "4–5–6" and players would respond, "We all we need." With all the injuries, this slogan was taking on an additional meaning. "We all we got" started to represent the remaining healthy players and "we all we need" stood for the next man up had to fill the void.

Losing Hicks would be a major blow for the defense. He was always in the middle of the action and found a way to be near the ball. Hicks had torn his left Achilles in college so he was familiar with the rehabilitation process.

"It's wild because my last one was a down-in-the-dumps rehab because I hadn't dedicated my life to Christ yet," Hicks said. "This rehab, I felt He was really trying to teach me something and allow me to prove that I was going to handle this one completely different. It's always hard in those times because all you see is the team and how you can impact and help the team and that is all you want to do. When you are on the sideline and hurt, you feel like you have let the team down in a way.

"I think what God was calling on my heart was where is my identity, you know? In the times of pain, in the times of hurt, why am I feeling this way? It was because a lot of me wanted to have my identity in football. I think He really taught me a lot of who I am in Him and what I am supposed to be doing in this world. How I am supposed to be acting in certain situations."

The injury allowed Hicks to realize his identity doesn't lie in his success as a player. God doesn't care about what we do for a living. He's concerned with what we do for the kingdom and who we are as people. For those who find their identity in Christ, He brings an incredible sense of peace—the kind of peace that's evident in Maragos and Hicks. Learning these lessons helped these guys find a way to be thankful through their adversity.

"I was lucky enough to have awesome believers around me," Hicks said. "We just constantly would get in there and talk about life in the locker room. Our lives changed. No doubt, no question we wished it would be the same, but we became leaders off the field, and it gave us a completely different perspective. When you are in season mode you got your blinders on and you're not looking sideways. It is straight ahead narrow focused. When you go from one hundred to nothing, completely zero like we did, we were able to see some things that guys that are playing aren't able to see, and I think we led in a different way and grew in a bunch of different areas of life. We were able to do it together, which we never wish upon anybody, but God was gracious with that."

Seeing the way the injured guys handled adversity inspired the rest of the team. Hicks was Zach Ertz's roommate on the road. They prayed together before every game and continued to do it by phone when Hicks couldn't travel.

"I would know what it is he was going through mentally and physically, but you could tell his main trust was still in the Lord even throughout everything he was going through," Ertz said. "I think even seeing that from afar, even though I lost my roommate on the road for most of the season, I was still able to see the Lord moving in him, and it had a profound impact not only on me but I think a lot of guys on the team."

Despite a rash of injuries to some of their top players, the Eagles kept on winning, and the victories started getting easier.

They finished October with a 33–10 romp over the winless San Francisco 49ers on a sloppy, rainy Sunday. Carson Wentz had two touchdown passes, including a 53-yard strike to Alshon Jeffery. Jalen Mills returned an interception 37 yards for a score. Zach Ertz flipped a ball he caught for a touchdown to baseball star Mike Trout, a lifelong Eagles fan who has season tickets behind the end zone. Six straight wins and a 7–1 start. Everyone around the league had taken notice. Fans in Philadelphia were starting to realize the team had potential to go a long way.

"It pretty much rained the whole game. It's going to maybe knock you off just a little bit with the weather, but guys really responded and did an outstanding job," Doug Pederson said. "And to score 33 like that, it was pretty impressive for them."

Next up was a visit from the Denver Broncos, a team that was struggling less than two years after winning a Super Bowl. Howie Roseman made a trade that week, acquiring running back Jay Ajayi from the Miami Dolphins for a fourth-round draft pick in 2018. Ajayi was a big boost to a rushing attack that was already ranked fifth in the league before his arrival. He was a Pro Bowl player just a year earlier when he ran for nearly 1,300 yards. But the Dolphins were willing to part ways with Ajayi, who had a reputation for being a selfish player. He went from a losing team to the one with the best record in the NFL. That helped him adjust to a decreased workload because Philadelphia used a rotation of running backs with LeGarrette Blount and Corey Clement.

"We do a lot of research on players before we trade for them," Roseman said. "Not only did we do a lot of research on a guy like this before, when he comes out in the draft, but we do that here before we make a deal. Really, in this league, you do business with people that you trust, and we feel like we have a good understanding of what was going on there. We also have a good understanding of what we have in our locker room and the chemistry that we have on this team. We weren't going to bring anyone here that would disrupt team chemistry. We feel very confident and comfortable about the player."

The London-born Ajayi with his black and blonde dreadlocks fit in nicely from the minute he arrived in Philly. He bought into Pederson's team-first approach and didn't show any signs of selfishness. Ajayi displayed his skills in his debut in front of the hometown crowd. Ajayi broke loose for a 46-yard touchdown run against the Broncos and finished with 77 yards rushing. Wentz threw four more touchdown passes. The Eagles routed Denver 51–23 to start November the way they left off the last month. They were 8–1 with a bye week coming up. Expectations were growing in Philadelphia. A city starving for a championship was getting more excited with each win. Pederson made sure he kept his players focused and grounded before they left for a few days of rest and relaxation.

"We've just got to continue to stay with the one-game mentality," Pederson said. "That's been a good formula for us this season. We can't get caught looking down the road at upcoming opponents and scenarios. That's for the media to speculate on and talk about. But we've just got to make sure that we maintain our focus, understand what got us to where we are and continue that process moving forward. I want the coaches and players to enjoy and to look back and reflect on what we've accomplished so far. As great as it is, we still have half a season and seven ball games left. If you don't take care of business from here on out, it's all for nothing."

The Eagles didn't need a reminder to come back ready for their next game. They were going to play the Dallas Cowboys on the road on *Sunday Night Football*. Philly fans hate the Cowboys more than any team in any other sport. Each week, diehard Eagles fans root for their favorite team and whoever is playing against Dallas. The Cowboys were the defending NFC East champions but already were three games behind Philadelphia. They desperately needed a win more than the Eagles and played like it in the first half, taking a 9–7 lead into the locker room.

But the Eagles dominated the second half, scoring 30 unanswered points in a runaway 37–9 victory. The offense didn't rely on Wentz, showing its balance as the rushing attack had 215 yards on the ground and two scores. Wentz also threw two touchdown passes.

"We just came out and got the running game going, so we just kind of relied on that," Wentz said. "That's just kind of the way our offense runs. Anybody every week can step up and just be that guy, and the way we can just be flexible and spread the ball around is what makes us hard to defend."

Thanksgiving had arrived, and the Eagles were blessed, thankful, and 9–1. The Chicago Bears and their rookie quarterback, Mitchell Trubisky, were no match for Philadelphia. Wentz fired three touchdown passes, and the defense thoroughly dominated the Bears in a 31–3 victory.

The winning streak had reached nine games and the games weren't even close anymore. Five straight wins were decided by a double-digit margin, four by at least 23 points and the last three by 28 points each. At 10–1, the Eagles had the best record in the NFL, but the Minnesota Vikings were right behind them in the NFC at 9–2. Fans were no longer thinking just playoffs. The Super Bowl didn't seem far-fetched. Instead, it was becoming part of the daily conversation on sports talk shows. The Eagles had ten wins in their first eleven games only three other times in franchise history. They played for the championship each time, winning it all in 1949 and losing the Super Bowl twice.

"I'm never really surprised by a lot, but any time in the National Football League you can win like that, that's big, because that's hard to do," Wentz said. "That's just a credit to the coaches and the guys just buying in. Every week we just come in ready to work. It doesn't matter who the opponent is or what their record is. It never really matters. It's just like we're going to win each day and get better each day. Then we just try to come out and enjoy it on game day. We're playing with a lot of momentum, a lot of energy, and a lot of swagger out there. The defense is playing unbelievable. We feed off of that, and they feed off of us. So it's a lot of fun right now."

Long before the season started, the Eagles had asked the NFL to schedule two of their three games on the West Coast on back-to-back weeks so they could do a long layover in California. The league obliged, giving the Eagles a three-game road trip to begin December. Seattle. Los Angeles. New York. The team planned to go to Anaheim, California, after playing the Seahawks to spend a week preparing to play the Rams by practicing in a baseball park at Angels Stadium, home of Eagles fan Mike Trout.

"This is a great opportunity for our football team. It's a great set of challenges for us," Pederson said before the Eagles embarked on a nine-day business trip.

It didn't start off well. The Eagles played their worst game of the season in prime time on *Sunday Night Football*. A 24–10 loss to the Seahawks that ended Philadelphia's nine-game winning streak. Russell Wilson had three touchdown passes while Carson Wentz made some costly mistakes. He threw for 348 yards, including an acrobatic 51-yard toss to Nelson Agholor on the run while falling forward. It probably would've been the highlight play of the season had the Eagles won the game. But Wentz overthrew Agholor on a likely touchdown earlier in the game and underthrew Agholor for another potential score. He also fumbled one yard away from the end zone and had an interception.

"We turned the ball over. They didn't," Wentz said. "On a road game like this, in this atmosphere against a great team like they are, it's tough to win when you do that. We will be fine. The guys in this locker room are all mature. We will all respond just fine. We are all frustrated about this one, but we're not too worried. I think we will be just fine."

The loss was a reality check, tempering some of the Super Bowl talk. The Vikings won a tough game on the road at Atlanta to move into a tie with Philadelphia for first place in the NFC at 10–2. The Rams were right behind the Eagles at 9–3 and ready to face them in Week 14. Another loss would drop Philadelphia into third place in the conference. It was going to be a pivotal game that would help decide playoff seeding. Every team wants to earn home-field advantage throughout the playoffs. The Eagles couldn't afford to slip up again.

CHAPTER TEN

UNANSWERED PRAYER

Zach Ertz knew something was wrong when Carson Wentz simply walked off the field after throwing a two-yard touchdown pass to Alshon Jeffery to give the Philadelphia Eagles a 31–28 lead over the Los Angeles Rams late in the third quarter of a highly anticipated game. No high-fives. No fist-bumps. Not even a smile. Wentz just walked slowly with a slight limp.

This was the first time Wentz and the Eagles faced Jared Goff and the Rams since the two quarterbacks were picked first and second in the 2016 draft. There was a long way to go before Wentz-Goff turned into a Tom Brady-Peyton Manning rivalry, but they were going head-to-head in a game that had strong playoff implications. The Eagles needed a victory to clinch the NFC East title and remain in first place in their quest to secure the No. 1 seed. The surprising Rams were 9–3 under rookie head coach Sean McVay and led the NFC West. They had already secured their first winning season since 2003 and were aiming for their first playoff berth since 2004.

Wentz threw an interception on the third play of the game and the Eagles quickly fell behind 7–0. But Wentz showed why he was the frontrunner for the NFL's Most Valuable Player award. He led the Eagles on three straight touchdown drives, tossing scoring passes to backup players.

With Ertz, one of the best tight ends in the league, sidelined by a concussion, Wentz didn't have his favorite target. Veteran Brent Celek and Trey Burton had an opportunity to fill in at his position, and Wentz got them involved right away. He fired a 5-yard touchdown pass to Celek to tie the game. Then Wentz made a perfect throw on third down, dropping the ball in between two defenders to Burton for a 20-yard touchdown pass that gave the Eagles a lead. His next touchdown pass again came on third down and again went to Burton for a leaping 11-yard score. The score was 21–7 less than five minutes into the second quarter. Wentz and the Eagles were making a statement that they were the best team in the conference. Doubters argued the level of competition the Eagles had faced to that point wasn't strong and pointed to the offense's struggles a week earlier in Seattle.

After spending a few days practicing in California, the Eagles were ready to prove they were a legitimate Super Bowl contender. They even got a pep talk two days before the game from former Los Angeles Lakers superstar Kobe Bryant, who grew up an Eagles fan in the Philadelphia suburbs. Doug Pederson said Bryant's message to the team centered on paying attention to details.

"Do your job, focus on your assignment, sort of have a bulldog-type mentality when you take the field, and to be aggressive, and just all the things that he's learned over his Hall-of-Fame career," Pederson said. "We have a lot of NBA fans on the team, coaches, players, and staff included, and have followed his career a long time. So just a great pleasure to have him speak and address the team."

But Goff and the Rams weren't going to quit just because they were down 21–7. Goff threw a pair of touchdown passes, and Blake Countess returned a punt 16 yards for a touchdown to give the Rams a 28–24 lead in the third quarter.

Now it was Wentz's turn to lead a comeback. He drove the Eagles down to the Rams 2-yard line, completing a pair of clutch passes on third down to extend the nearly eight-minute drive.

Then, it happened. The moment every Eagles fan feared.

Wentz dropped back to pass from the 2. He didn't see an open receiver so he took off running the way he always does, trying to make a play happen with his legs. His scrambling ability was a major reason why Philadelphia's offense had so much success. Wentz got outside the pocket, turned the corner, and saw an open lane. He dove into the end zone, hurling his body in the air and was sandwiched between two tacklers. Touchdown. Wait. Hold on. A referee had thrown a yellow flag. It didn't count. A holding penalty on Lane Johnson negated the score. But that wasn't the worst news. Wentz got up limping.

"It was a fluke hit," Wentz said. "When I got up and walked back to the huddle, it felt unstable."

On the radio broadcast, longtime Eagles play-by-play announcer Merrill Reese said, "The one Eagle you can least afford to lose."

It couldn't be a serious injury, though. Wentz didn't stay down. He didn't have a trainer look at it. He wasn't carted off the field. He wasn't even helped off. He simply walked gingerly back to the huddle and stayed in the game.

Wentz handed the ball to Corey Clement on the next two

plays and he ran it to the 2-yard line. On third down, Wentz's pass to Jeffery was incomplete. It was fourth down and Pederson went for it because he had confidence in his offense to regain the lead instead of kicking a short field goal.

Wentz took a one-step drop, looked to his right and pump-faked. He turned his eyes to the left and tossed a pass just before a rusher got through a blocker. The ball was low but exactly where it had to go to avoid the traffic. Jeffery reached down and scooped it with his fingertips before the ball hit the ground.

Jeffery jumped up and down while teammates ran over to celebrate with him. But Wentz just walked off the field with a blank expression. He went inside the blue privacy tent on the sideline and trainers came over to check him out. His left knee was injured, and it appeared serious. Doctors sent him back to the locker room for further testing, and the team announced to the media that Wentz wouldn't return to the game.

Television cameras followed Wentz on the long walk back to the tunnel. People watching at home or listening on the radio and the large group of Eagles fans who made the trip to Los Angeles for the game still had hope. Wentz walked on his own power. He didn't need crutches or any assistance.

"My mind was all over the place," he said, recalling his thoughts at that moment. "How long would I be out? Would it be one game or the rest of the season?"

Ertz watched everything unfold from the sideline and wanted to help his friend.

"Carson's an unbelievable competitor," Ertz said. "But when he is out there you can tell something is wrong because he is a guy that doesn't show any emotion on the field let alone pain being that emotion. He just kept kind of pointing to his knee, pointing to his knee and shaking his head. So he throws the touchdown, and he just walks off the field slowly. He's a guy that is always jogging everywhere. So he is slowly walking off, and he goes into the tent. I go over there, standing over there kind of waiting for him. He comes out and I was like, "Dude, are you okay?" And he was just like, 'Something's wrong, something's wrong.' And at that point I knew something was not right with him not only physically, but he didn't know how to go through it mentally too. I was next to Trey [Burton] and he said: 'Why don't you just go in with Carson? We don't need you out here.'"

Ertz jogged after Wentz and followed him into the locker room. He contacted Jordan Hicks and Pastor Kyle Horner and decided to lay hands on Wentz.

"It was just a moment that God knew Carson was going to need someone that day," Ertz said. "He knew what I was dealing with and just put us in a situation where we could be with each other with our brother. When I saw what he was going through, I put everything I was going through aside. The first thing I thought of when this happened was I texted Jordan, I texted Kyle and got Kyle on the phone, and we put our hand on Carson's knee and prayed for healing."

Meanwhile, on the field, the Eagles were suddenly losing the game and facing life without Wentz for at least the fore-seeable future. Goff led the Rams on a go-ahead scoring drive. Trailing 35–31, Nick Foles replaced Wentz at quarterback. Foles had thrown just four passes the entire season, but management brought him back to Philadelphia for this reason. They wanted a capable backup in case Wentz went down.

Foles kept the offense moving in the fourth quarter. He made clutch passes and set up Jake Elliott for a pair of field goals to give the Eagles a 37–35 lead. The defense scored a touchdown on the final play to seal a 43–35 victory that clinched the NFC East title for the Eagles.

Despite his injury, Wentz was there waiting to congratulate his teammates and give them high-fives and handshakes when they returned to the locker room.

"I'm excited we're NFC champs, but it's emotional," Foles said. "The guy you work with every day, you think the world of, I think he's the MVP, it's not easy, but I know this team will step up and rally no matter what, so we'll see what will happen from here. I'm absolutely ready, that's why I'm here. I'm ready to go. Prepare every day, work every day, so I'm ready to go if need be."

Pederson gathered the team in the locker room after the game and congratulated them on an impressive, resilient win.

"Great team effort. Now that we got this out of the way," Pederson said, pointing to an NFC East champions cap on offensive lineman Halapoulivaati Vaitai's head. "We got three left. We're playing for something bigger now, boys. It's gonna take everybody in the room to dig in, dig in, dig in these next few weeks. I'm so proud of you, guys."

Wentz left Los Angeles Memorial Coliseum with his left knee wrapped in a brace. A cart drove him up the tunnel out of the stadium, and he hobbled into one of the team buses. Wentz was scheduled for an MRI on Monday. The best-case scenario would've been a severe sprain instead of a torn anterior cruciate ligament. Everyone hoped and prayed that the original diagnosis was wrong.

God didn't answer that prayer. Wentz had a torn ACL. The Eagles had to move forward without him. But God had a greater plan.

"Obviously, it didn't happen, but that doesn't make it less powerful," Ertz said. "At the end of the day, His will be done. We can pray. We can do that, but we trust Him regardless of the outcome because of how much we love Him."

CHAPTER ELEVEN

WE ALL WE GOT, WE ALL WE NEED

The mood in the locker room after the Eagles beat the Rams to improve to 11–2 and win the NFC East division was somber because of Carson Wentz's injury. They already saw several of their best players suffer season-ending knee injuries. Darren Sproles. Chris Maragos. Jason Peters. Jordan Hicks. They couldn't afford to lose their franchise quarterback too. Wentz was the man who got them to this point. He led the NFL with thirty-three touchdown passes, a franchise record for a single season. He made dynamic plays with his legs. He was the favorite to win the NFL MVP award. How could the Eagles survive losing their best player?

Malcolm Jenkins wanted to make sure the team didn't sulk and didn't lose its confidence. The Eagles had just checked off their first goal: division championship. There was far more to accomplish. Jenkins had become the vocal team leader. He was the guy who delivered passionate post-game speeches and offered encouragement and words of wisdom whenever he felt necessary. He knew he had to keep his teammates focused on winning the Super Bowl. After Doug Pederson addressed the team, it was time for Jenkins to speak his mind. This would be the most important talk of the season. As usual, Jenkins was fired-up. He didn't hold back in a colorful talk.

"We said, we all we got, we all we need. Believe that," Jenkins said, emphasizing that the team needs to rally around whoever is on the field and play with confidence. "We got bigger goals. So we get back to work man, you know what's in our minds bro—championships and that's it. Nothing short of that, no excuses."

With Wentz out, the Eagles needed to stick to their "we all we got, we all we need" mantra more than ever now. Pederson confirmed at his Monday news conference that the MRI on Wentz's knee revealed he indeed had torn his ACL and would require season-ending surgery.

"Can your team overcome this?" was the first question Pederson was asked by a reporter after delivering the news.

"It sure can, heck yeah," Pederson said before listing all the players who already had been hurt. "This is no different. Yeah, he is the quarterback of our football team. Each one of these guys that I mentioned is tough to replace. But you know what, the reason we went out and got Nick Foles was for reasons like this and situations like this. I'm excited for Nick. I hate it for Carson Wentz. I hate it for the career, the season, that he's been having. But at the same time, it's been the next-man-up mentality, and that's how we approach it."

December 11 was a rough day in Philadelphia. Two weeks before Christmas, Eagles fans were miserable. Some literally cried after they heard the news. They mourned Wentz's injury like a death in the family. Most fans assumed their Super Bowl dreams were destroyed. They blamed Pederson for calling a pass from the 2-yard line instead of a run on the play Wentz got hurt. Some even wanted the team to sign Colin Kaepernick because they didn't believe Foles could do the job. Full disclosure: I thought Kaepernick would've been a solid backup behind Foles. He has the talent to be a starting quarterback in the NFL and threw sixteen touchdowns versus only four interceptions in his last season in 2016 while playing for a terrible team—Chip Kelly's 2–14 San Francisco 49ers. But the Eagles didn't sign another quarterback, because they were confident in Foles and backup Nate Sudfeld. I also declared that week on the NFL podcast that I hosted for The Associated Press that Foles would lead the Eagles to the Super Bowl and lose to Tom Brady and the New England Patriots. I had confidence in Foles because he proved himself in 2013. His struggles in St. Louis in 2015 were more about poor coaching and lack of talent around him. The 2017 Eagles were set up to win with Foles because the offense had a strong supporting cast, the defense was excellent, and the coaching staff was sharp.

Pederson encouraged people to believe in the team.

"To the fans out there, you can't lose faith," he said. "This has been a resilient football team all season long. If there's ever an opportunity for me as a head football coach to rally the troops, now might be the time. We just came off a tremendous victory to win the NFC East. Guys are riding extremely high. It's a little bittersweet. But we got the Giants this week. We got an opportunity that if you win Sunday, you get a first-round bye.

"So there is still a lot to play for. That's what's exciting about the rest of this season. We're still playing for that opportunity to hopefully be in that game. Nick has played a ton of football. I was

we drafted him, and we drafted him for a reason. Then
ut and got him again this offseason for a reason. You
it it to be under these circumstances, but at the same
time, my confidence is extremely high in Nick. You saw what he
did [against the Rams]. I've got confidence in Nick. I've got confidence in the guys. That's what I'm going to continue to do. I'm
going to continue to stay aggressive. I'm going to lead this football
team. It falls more on my shoulders than it does these players.
That's why they need to stay encouraged. That's why they need to
stay excited about this opportunity we have in front of us."

This wasn't simply typical coachspeak. Pederson truly
believed what he was saying. He wouldn't allow negativity to
infiltrate his team. And Wentz couldn't allow negative thoughts
to pollute his mind. He faced his toughest test yet. How would
he respond to this adversity? Anyone who wondered why God
allowed bad things to happen to good people surely asked this
question now. How could this injury happen at this time to such
a loyal disciple?

But the truth is that Christians aren't immune to trials and
tribulations. The Bible is filled with stories about faithful ser-
vants enduring far worse than a torn knee ligament. Job lost all
his children. His body was afflicted with pain. He was a tortured
soul, yet he never turned against God. Paul was thrown in jail
for preaching the gospel. He also suffered physical abuse and still
spread the Good News through all the calamities.

Wentz boldly proclaimed his love for Christ in good times.
On his worst day as a professional athlete, he didn't waver.

"Obviously, it's been a rough day for me personally. I'm not
going to lie," Wentz said in a video posted on social media the
day after he was injured. "I have a ton of faith in the Lord and in

His plan, but at the end of day it's still been a tough one. And it will be tough on me for a little bit. As I just kind of reflect tonight, I just know the Lord's working through it. I know Jesus has a plan through it. I know He's trying to grow me into something, teach me something, use me somehow, some way."

Foles sympathized with his friend. He genuinely felt bad for Wentz, even though it meant he would now have an opportunity to play.

"We put in a lot of work this season, a lot of work. We've won a lot of games. It has been a great team effort," Foles said. "Carson has been a big piece of that puzzle. When you have your starting quarterback go down, it's emotional. It's emotional for me. I work with him every day. We do everything together. I'm dealing emotionally with seeing him go down. You never want that."

Our toughest test often becomes our testimony. But this wasn't going to be easy for Wentz or his teammates. Many players were still struggling with the news when they gathered for their weekly Bible study with Pastor Ted Winsley. Several of the injured guys were regulars at these sessions.

"It was shook," Winsley said of the atmosphere in the room. "They started connecting the dots. Jordan Matthews gets traded. Chris Maragos, Caleb Sturgis, Jordan Hicks go down. Guys said, 'Are we cursed?' I said, 'No! But we have an enemy, and we identified ourselves as an enemy to the enemy, and didn't Jesus say, "In this life you will have tribulation but be in good cheer because I have overcome."

Players began to realize perhaps there was a greater plan. Nick Foles was no ordinary backup. He went to the Pro Bowl in 2013 after having one of the best statistical seasons in NFL history. He led the Eagles to the NFC East title that season, the team's last playoff appearance. Things didn't go his way for a few years, but the Eagles really wanted him back in case Wentz got hurt. Foles was a brother in Christ, a strong believer who put faith and family first. Maybe it was his time to shine.

"We know God didn't get people injured," Winsley said. "We know it wasn't His will, but we know God is omniscient so God knows everything. He's not some sadistic dude with a magnifying glass making bad things happen, but the other part is, He has a plan that is greater than ours if we will submit to it. Romans 8:28 says: 'And we know that in all things God works for the good of those who love him, who have been called according to his purpose.' So for the guys who do believe and the fact that Nick came back, is it a coincidence, if we have to depend on somebody, it would be Nick? Guys were able to see God is still in this. He hasn't left us to fail. It looks like He set us up to believe and it kept building."

CHAPTER TWELVE

HUMILITY THAT WINS

I remember asking Nick Foles for his favorite Bible verse during his second season in the NFL. It perfectly summed up his character. "Humble yourselves, therefore, under God's mighty hand, that he may lift you up in due time," Foles said, quoting 1 Peter 5:6.

Foles explained that he started reading the Bible at a young age, and this verse had stuck with him. He credited his parents for teaching him to be humble regardless of his situation. They also taught him to give his teammates and coaches credit for his success.

"My goal is to always stay humble, to always be gracious, and always be thankful for everything I have because we never know what's going to happen the next day," Foles said.

Foles grew up in a hardworking family living in Austin, Texas. His parents, Larry and Melissa Foles, were restaurateurs. In 2011, they sold their Eddie V's restaurant chain for $59 million. But success didn't come easy. Larry Foles worked countless hours over many years to build his fortune. He instilled in his children, Nick, Lacey, and Katie, the value of a strong work ethic and responsibility.

"We didn't have the easiest life growing up," Nick Foles said. "And for him and my mom to give me an opportunity to play this game, to provide for us as kids, to watch him go through adversity throughout his entire life and overcome it—he didn't even graduate high school. And he's been very successful in his career path, and I got to watch him as a young kid come home at midnight, smelling like a kitchen because he was working in a kitchen. Trying to get into the restaurant business isn't easy. Trying to start it up, he lost everything. But to watch him as a kid just continue to give me an opportunity to play, and I never really realized it until I got older how much he worked, how much him and my mom sacrificed for me and my two younger sisters."

Nick was a two-sport star at Westlake High School, which was located in an affluent neighborhood in Travis County, west of Austin. Drew Brees, the New Orleans Saints star quarterback and future Hall of Famer, went to Westlake a decade earlier and led the team to a state championship in 1996. Foles broke several of Brees's passing records, but his team lost the state title game his senior year. Foles played through a torn rotator cuff in his throwing shoulder that season, and he saw his friend's football career cut short after he had a cardiac arrest episode during a game. Foles also starred for three seasons on the basketball team and was recruited by Georgetown and a few other schools to play hoops. He chose football and Arizona State but later changed his mind and went to Michigan State for one year. Foles then transferred to the University of Arizona and was the starter for three seasons. He led the Pac-12 Conference in passing as a senior.

Despite prolific passing numbers, scouts weren't sold on him coming out of college. Foles had the size—6-foot-6, 243 pounds—and arm strength that teams love. But he lacked speed and was labeled a pocket passer who wouldn't be able to improvise and make plays with his legs. Foles ran the 40-yard dash in 5.14 seconds at the NFL draft combine, the slowest of all quarterbacks in attendance. They considered him, at best, a game-manager, a term used to describe quarterbacks who didn't have much upside.

Six quarterbacks were selected in the 2012 draft before the Eagles chose Foles in the third round with the eighty-eighth overall pick. Andy Reid, who was the coach at the time, had his eyes on Russell Wilson. He went to the Seattle Seahawks at pick No. 75 and became one of the best players in the league. Kirk Cousins was still on the draft board when the Eagles chose Foles. Some members of Philadelphia's scouting department preferred Cousins, but Reid had final say. Cousins went to the Washington Redskins in the fourth round. He eventually replaced Robert Griffin III and thrived. In March 2018, Cousins signed a three-year, $84 million fully guaranteed contract with the Minnesota Vikings, the first contract of its kind in NFL history.

Reid viewed Foles as a future starter, someone he could develop over time. Reid knew something about quarterbacks. He worked with Hall of Famer Brett Favre in Green Bay and Donovan McNabb in Philadelphia. He also coached Michael Vick during the best season of his career with the Eagles in 2010. If Andy Reid sees potential in a quarterback, you should bet on him. Vick was still the starter when Foles arrived in Philly. But the injury-prone Vick got hurt, giving Foles an opportunity to start six games as a rookie. The Eagles lost five of them. They lost plenty of games that season. A 4–12 record cost Reid his job. Chip Kelly replaced him, bringing an up-tempo offense, sports science, and other innovative ideas to the league.

Foles went to training camp in the summer of 2013 competing with Vick for the starting job. Vick seemed like a better fit for the way Kelly wanted to run his offense. He was arguably the most dynamic quarterback ever to play the game. On any given play, Vick could throw a perfect spiral 70 yards downfield with a simple flick of his left wrist, or break away from tacklers and sprint 70 yards for a score. Both quarterbacks played well in the preseason, but Vick won the job. So Foles patiently waited for an opportunity. When Vick injured his hamstring in a game against the New York Giants in early October, Foles took over and never looked back. He flourished. In his third start that season at Oakland on November 3, Foles threw seven touchdown passes against the Raiders to tie an NFL record. Only six players had ever done it before and one more—Drew Brees—has done it since.

Foles kept firing touchdown passes, proving he didn't need speed or scrambling skills to thrive in Kelly's offense. Foles led the Eagles to the NFC East championship, went to the Pro Bowl, and was offensive MVP in that all-star game. His season stats looked like a typo: twenty-nine touchdown passes (including playoffs) and only two interceptions. His touchdown-interception ratio was the best in NFL history. His passer rating (119.0) was third-best.

Even though Foles and the Eagles lost to Brees and the Saints in the playoffs, it seemed Philadelphia had found its franchise quarterback. Foles, by the way, walked off the field with a lead in that wild-card playoff game against New Orleans, but the defense blew it.

Expectations were high for Foles and the Eagles entering the 2014 season. Of course, there were critics too. Many people wondered if his sensational sophomore season was an aberration. Some of the silliest critiques centered on Foles's personality. One writer said in a magazine profile piece that Foles was too nice and too unselfish to lead the team to a Super Bowl title. Foles was all of those things. But he was a winner too.

Success didn't change Foles. He didn't care about self-promotion or marketing opportunities. Faith. Family. Football. Those were his priorities in that order.

"I still am the same guy y'all talked to when I arrived here my rookie year," Foles said in April 2014. "There's opportunities that arise, but you also have to learn to say no to different things. My most important thing is my faith and my family. That's what I worry about the most. If things are taking time away from my family, I gotta say no and obviously, I've got to be the best football player I can be to provide for them."

Foles had the best season of his football career in 2013, but he faced adversity off the field. His then-girlfriend, Tori Moore, was diagnosed with Postular Orthostatic Tachycardia Syndrome (POTS) and later learned she had Lyme disease. The couple met after Foles transferred to Arizona, and they were friends at first. Tori played volleyball while Nick focused on football. They began a long-distance relationship after finishing school. Nick went to Philadelphia, and Tori went to Portland to work for Nike. Their lives changed after she became ill. Her condition would cause her heart rate to rise thirty beats per minute just from sitting or standing. The couple spent a difficult month together at the Mayo Clinic in Rochester, Minnesota, in February 2014 trying to get a handle on her diagnosis.

"We got engaged while we were at the Mayo Clinic. We got married at a courthouse two months later, because we knew we were in for a run," Foles said. "We never had a wedding ceremony. We never had a honeymoon. Just the journey we've gone on and gone through, and just to see her strength and to see her determination and to see her health continue to improve, and she still deals with it, it's amazing. It gives me strength because I know she deals with it every single day."

———————————

For the first time as a professional, Foles was entrenched as the starting quarterback entering the 2014 season. The Eagles had signed Mark Sanchez to be the backup and provide insurance. Foles was undoubtedly the No. 1 guy. Sanchez's career had spiraled downward after he led the New York Jets to consecutive appearances in the AFC championship game his first two seasons in the NFL in 2009–10. A fresh start in Philadelphia could revive his career.

Foles led the Eagles to three straight wins to start the season but he wasn't quite as sharp playing behind an injury-riddled offensive line. He tossed two interceptions in the first two games, matching his entire total from 2013. The personal stats didn't matter as long as the team was winning. The Eagles were 5–2 entering the eighth game of the season at Houston. Foles threw a long touchdown pass and a Pick-6 in the first quarter. Then he took a hard shot from Texans linebacker Whitney Mercilus. Broken collarbone. Season over. Sanchez replaced Foles, and the team went 4–4 the rest of the way. They missed the playoffs despite winning ten games. Chip Kelly got control of personnel decisions from Howie Roseman. And things unraveled.

Days before the start of the NFL's free agency period in 2015,

Foles and his wife were baptized by Pastor Ted Winsley at the Pro Athletes Outreach Conference in San Diego. Water baptism symbolizes a new beginning in Christ. Foles was about to get a fresh start in football too. On March 13, the first day of the league season, Foles was traded to the St. Louis Rams for quarterback Sam Bradford. It was one of a series of stunning moves by Kelly. Bradford had missed the entire 2014 season after tearing his left ACL for the second consecutive year. The Rams were eager to move the former No. 1 overall pick. They considered Foles someone they could build around. Before he even threw his first pass in St. Louis, Foles signed a two-year contract extension that included $14 million guaranteed. The Rams were coming off eight straight losing seasons, but coach Jeff Fisher was confident Foles would help them end that streak.

In Philadelphia, Foles was 14–4 in games he started. He was also the team's spiritual leader, inheriting the role after Jason Avant left the team. He had an impact on Sanchez, who dedicated his life to Christ after joining the Eagles.

"When Nick got traded, Sanchez called me and said, 'I've been watching Nick. I'm ready to step up, whatever you want me to do, I'm willing to be a leader spiritually,'" Winsley recalled. "Players leave but the culture they leave behind is strong."

Foles had an impressive debut with the Rams, leading them to a 34–31 victory over the defending NFC champion Seattle Seahawks in Week 1. He threw for 297 yards and one touchdown. He was so-so in the next two games—both losses. But he had another excellent performance in Week 4. Foles completed 67 percent of his passes for three touchdowns in a 24–22 win over Arizona. It was downhill from there. Foles threw only two touchdown passes and nine interceptions over the next seven games. The Rams lost five of them. Fisher benched Foles for Case Keenum in December, but the team's problems weren't the quarterback. When the Rams moved to Los Angeles after the season, they traded up to acquire the No. 1 pick. It was clear Foles was no longer in their plans. He asked the team to release him after quarterback Jared Goff was drafted first overall.

Fisher, who was still the Rams coach, finally granted Foles his wish right before training camp in a phone call that was recorded by television cameras for the HBO series *Hard Knocks*. It was an embarrassing way to end Foles' brief tenure with the Rams. His experience with St. Louis/Los Angeles nearly led him to quit playing.

———————

At age twenty-seven, Nick Foles was ready to retire from the NFL. He hadn't picked up a football for eight months. His love for the game was gone.

"I just didn't have that joy. It was scary to me," Foles said. "Growing up in Texas, I always played football since I was a kid. It was tough, but going through it was the greatest thing in the world."

Foles turned to God for guidance. He drew inspiration from 2 Corinthians 12:9: "My grace is sufficient for you, for my power is made perfect in weakness."

"I kept reading Scripture, I kept praying, I kept asking God. So many of us ask God for signs; we ask God, 'Hey, please just put it on the wall, like, I want to know,' but that's not how it works," Foles said. "He's not always going to do that. He was shaping me. He was bringing me down to my knees. At that moment, through that prayer, He said, 'Hey, just take a step of faith. You're either going to stop playing the game of football, and you're going to go on to a different area of your life and I'm going to be with you, I'm going to be the most important thing in your life, or you're going to step back into football, and you're going to continue to play, and I'm going to be with you every step of the way, and you're going to play to glorify me."

Foles was a free agent for the first time in his career. He went to California for a few days on a camping and fly-fishing trip to clear his mind and think about his future. When he returned, several teams had contacted his agent. One team stood out because of its coach. Andy Reid offered him an opportunity to be a backup in Kansas City, so Foles prayed about it with his wife and sought advice from his parents.

"It was an opportunity where I would go to be around someone I respect and love," Foles said. "Coach Reid was the guy who drafted me as a rookie. He's a guy that I always stayed in touch with, always thought the world of. So as I sort of just stepped away from the game for those few days, I was able to talk to him about how I felt. It really was only Coach Reid. That was it. I really didn't care about any other offer. I told my agents, 'That's the guy I want to play for.'"

Foles signed a contract with the Chiefs on August 5, 2016. By his fourth day in training camp, his joy had returned.

"The emotions were unreal," he said. "It wasn't an easy decision. It's not like it was 100 percent, but my faith and my guidance and the way I felt going into that experience allowed me to grow, to make me a better player now because you experience those emotions, you go through that. It's an emotional thing. It's something I've done my entire life, and to go through that and make that decision, that wasn't easy. But I leaned on my wife, I leaned on my family, and I leaned on my faith in those moments, and I'm very grateful I made the decision I did and we made it together.

"It took a lot more faith to come back and play than it would've to go in the other direction. Either way would've been fine. Either way, I would've trusted in God. I would've done something else and glorified God in that instance. The reason I decided to come back is I've loved the game of football since I was a kid, I loved playing sports, I loved being part of a team, and I knew as a person that the more growth I've had and the more opportunity I would have to glorify God and trust in Him would be to go back and play football."

Foles also took a leap of faith that summer by registering for online graduate classes at Liberty University's Rawlings School of Divinity. He felt a calling to minister to high school students after spending time talking to them at various appearances over the years. It's a passion that may eventually lead him to become a pastor.

"I wanted to continue to learn and challenge my faith. It's a challenge because you are writing papers that are biblically correct," he said. "You want to impact people's hearts. When I speak to [students], that's such a time of young men and young women's lives that there's a lot of things that are thrown at them, so much temptation in this world, so much going on with social media and the internet that you want to talk to them and address it and share all the weaknesses I have because I've fallen many times. It's something I want to do. I can't play football forever. I've been blessed with an amazing platform and it's just a door God has opened, but I still have a lot of school left and a long journey."

Foles rediscovered his passing touch in Kansas City. He filled in for the second half after Alex Smith suffered a concussion in a mid-season game against Indianapolis and played well. He started the next game against Jacksonville and looked like the old Nick Foles. After the season, however, the Chiefs declined to exercise an option to renew his contract. Once again, Foles became a free agent.

The Eagles wanted to bring him back to Philadelphia, but Chase Daniel was already Carson Wentz's backup, and the team still owed him $5 million for 2017. Howie Roseman called Jeffrey Lurie to make sure he was willing to sign off on a decision to cut Daniel and sign Foles to a contract that included $7 million in guarantees.

"I remember the phone call," Lurie recalled. "Howie said, 'We have an opportunity to do this. Do you have any reservations of using this $12 million this way versus other positions?' And we both agreed this was absolutely the right thing to do. Our priority is to make sure we have the very best possible other starting quarterback. I won't even call Nick a backup, because we had him evaluated as a very strong quarterback."

It turned out to be one of the best decisions the Philadelphia Eagles ever made.

CHAPTER
THIRTEEN

CARSON'S TEAM

Carson Wentz, Nick Foles, and Nate Sudfeld formed a special bond in their first season with the Eagles. The three quarterbacks prayed together, listened to worship music while watching film, and helped each other become better players and better men. There was no jealousy or backstabbing, no hoping the other guy gets injured. Just three guys who love Jesus, love football, and love each other.

"Our faith unites us," Foles said. "I'm grateful we all have spent so much time together developing that relationship."

Sudfeld joined the team right before the first week of the season after he was cut by the Washington Redskins. As the son and grandson of preachers, he fit right in with Wentz and Foles.

"They're honestly like brothers to me," Sudfeld said.

Sudfeld has been on mission trips to Romania and several to Africa. His grandparents, Bob and Charlene Pagett, are the founders of Assist International, a second-generation nonprofit that seeks to address the needs of the developing world. His father, Ralph Sudfeld, is the current CEO, and his mother, Michelle Sudfeld, is Director of Administration. Naturally, Nate joined Wentz on a trip to Haiti after the season. When Wentz went down, Foles and Sudfeld were sure to lift his spirits and encourage him.

"As a teammate, someone who cares a lot about him, you hurt, but you're there to support him, pray for him," Foles said. "Carson is such a huge part of this organization and will be for a long time, and he's done so much for this team on the field and in the locker room. My job now is to step in that huddle and keep this thing rolling, and that's what I plan on doing."

Former Eagles offensive coordinator Frank Reich is a fellow Christian who went to seminary school after a fourteen-year career in the NFL and later became the pastor of Covenant Presbyterian Church in Charlotte, North Carolina. Reich appreciated the brotherhood among the quarterbacks he coached in 2017.

"That's a tight-knit room. The three of those guys are really close," Reich said. "Our primary calling in life as Christians is to bring out the best in other people. That's the primary message of Christianity. We've been created to glorify God. He gives us gifts and abilities, and we're supposed to bring those out in other people."

Shortly after he had surgery just three days after suffering his injury, Wentz FaceTimed his quarterback buddies. He was ordering a burger and still feeling the effects from anesthesia but wanted to check in.

"The first question he asks: 'So what's this new play I saw in the emails,'" Sudfeld said. "I was like, 'You sure you want to know right now?' He was feeling pretty loopy. It was funny. Classic Carson."

On the field, it was all business. Foles was preparing for his first start against the woeful New York Giants, a team that was

2–11 and had just fired head coach Ben McAdoo and general manager Jerry Reese.

Eagles fans were in a state of depression because Wentz was hurt. Football analysts no longer considered Philadelphia the team to beat in the NFC. But Reich and Doug Pederson had real confidence in Foles. Both men were career backups in the NFL. They understood what it takes to prepare to take over a team. They knew Foles could do it. Reich spent ten of his fourteen seasons playing behind Hall of Famer Jim Kelly in Buffalo. Filling in for an injured Kelly, he led the Bills to an incredible comeback against the Houston Oilers in an AFC wild-card playoff game on January 3, 1993. Down 35–3 in the third quarter, Reich rallied the Bills to a 41–38 overtime victory.

"The good thing with Nick is he's been there, done that," Reich said. "When I had an opportunity to step in and play, I had never done all the things that Nick had done as a starter. Nick knows he needs to just go be himself. One of the great things, anybody that knows Nick, knows he's very, very comfortable in his own skin and is very confident in his own abilities and is an excellent quarterback. And he exudes that confidence where the guys on this team see that, they feel that. You just know this guy's been successful. Just look at what he's done."

Pederson was the quarterbacks coach for the Eagles on Andy Reid's staff when Foles was a rookie. He saw him grow and mature as a leader and in his knowledge of the offense and reading a defense.

"We always knew he was a very smart, intellectual quarterback and could process information, but he's been able to take it to the next level in his preparation and just how he responds to the guys and how the guys have responded to him," Pederson said.

"He comes in and nobody blinks. Nobody bats an eye. There was no hesitation and that's just the confidence that the guys have in Nick."

Perhaps the defense didn't get the memo or they were feeling a bit weary after all that traveling and spending nine days in Seattle and California because they didn't show up in the first quarter against the Giants. Eli Manning led the offense to three straight scores to start the game, tossing a pair of touchdown passes. The Giants had a 20–7 lead less than two minutes into the second quarter.

But Foles wouldn't be outdone by Manning, the two-time Super Bowl MVP. He fired a touchdown pass to Zach Ertz and another one to Trey Burton to give Philly a lead. After the Giants went ahead in the third quarter, Jake Elliott kicked a field goal, Foles threw a touchdown pass to Nelson Agholor, and the Eagles held on for a 34–29 victory that secured a bye in the first-round of the playoffs.

Four touchdown passes, no turnovers for Foles. Everyone had to admit it was a pretty impressive first start. He even looked like Wentz on a play where he ducked away from New York's Jason Pierre-Paul and threw a deep ball that drew a pass interference penalty.

"It's huge just getting back out there playing a full game, on the road, in New York, NFC East, it doesn't matter what's going on in the season or what, it's always going to be a battle," Foles said. "We stuck together and we had some adversity early so it was a great game to come out and get a win."

NFC East title. Check. First-round bye. Check.

With two games remaining in the regular season, the Eagles had one more goal to cross off their to-do list. They were 12–2 and needed one more win to clinch the No. 1 seed in the NFC and secure home-field advantage throughout the playoffs. The Oakland Raiders were next up on the schedule. They were coming to Philly for *Monday Night Football* on Christmas. A season that began with Super Bowl aspirations for the Raiders dissolved quickly. At 6–8, they had nothing to play for but pride against the Eagles.

In the week leading up to the game, Foles made it clear he had no illusions about taking Wentz's job in the future. He emphasized that he understood his role was the backup quarterback and he was filling in until Wentz was ready to return.

"This is Carson's team," Foles said. "I respect Carson Wentz. I love that guy. I work with him every day, and I'm going to give him that respect because he is the franchise quarterback. My job right now is to lead these guys on the field as the starting quarterback, and I am going to do that. I've been here. I've done that. I know what it entails. I know the responsibility. But this is Carson Wentz's team. I respect him too much to make that statement. My mentality is when I step on that field, let's roll. I don't need to be named the starting quarterback."

Doug Pederson broke game-day tradition on Christmas morning and gave the players and coaches time to spend at home with their families before reporting for meetings and final preparations.

"You don't get these times back. You don't get them back," he said. "It's too important to me, my family. I want to make sure these players with young kids, coaches with young kids, they get a chance to spend Christmas morning together."

After unwrapping presents with their families and celebrating our Savior's birth, it was time for business on a cold, blustery night at Lincoln Financial Field. The temperature was 29 degrees with winds gusting at 15 miles per hour at kickoff. The conditions affected both quarterbacks. Neither Foles nor Derek Carr were accurate. Both misfired on many passes into the swirling wind. Foles threw a short screen pass for a touchdown, had one interception that bounced off Zach Ertz's hands, and was lucky another ball that should've been a Pick-6 was dropped by the defender. But Foles made the clutch throws late in the fourth quarter to lead the Eagles to a 19–10 victory that wrapped up the No. 1 seed for the first time since 2004.

"I didn't play good enough," Foles said. "I have to play cleaner and, obviously, play better. I'll look at the film. I'll improve."

One poor game by Foles gave doubters all the ammunition they needed to say, "I told you so."

Pederson wasn't concerned. "Everything is fixable, and everything is correctable. He'll learn from it. We'll learn from it," he said.

The biggest question heading into the final game of the regular season against the Dallas Cowboys was whether Foles would even play. Pederson had to weigh the risk of possibly losing Foles to an injury in a game that had no effect on the standings versus the need to give him more repetitions with the starting unit. After careful consideration, Pederson decided Foles and most of the regulars would start. Foles missed the entire preseason because of an elbow injury so Pederson felt more repetitions with the first-team offense was important to get him more comfortable.

"I don't want to not play them, and then it's three weeks later that they're playing a game," Pederson said. "I think that's foolish on my part. I want to make sure they stay into the moment. At the same time, I will be smart with how much they play, how long they play, and go from there."

Pederson ended up playing it safe. He rested some of his key players and only kept Foles and most of the other starters in for one quarter on a frigid New Year's Eve day. The Cowboys won 6–0, preventing the Eagles from earning a franchise-record fourteenth regular-season victory. Foles only threw eleven passes in the game and again didn't look sharp. However, Torrey Smith dropped a pass from Foles on the first offensive series that could've gone for a touchdown. Sudfeld played the final three quarters and showed some of the skills that impressed coaches in practice throughout the season. He completed 19 of 23 passes for 134 yards in his first career game.

"I've still got a lot confidence in our offense," Pederson said. "Again, it's not one person or one guy. It's tough in this situation where you know you're kind of maybe only going to get a quarter, maybe a couple series, and you're coming out. But I've still got a lot of confidence in the guys."

In Philadelphia, it was full panic mode. Fickle fans and hot-take media folks said Sudfeld should start in the playoffs. Some writers looking to write those click-bait stories tried to create a quarterback controversy. Pederson made it clear Foles was his starter. But he didn't rule out the possibility he would consider benching Foles if he struggled again.

"It's a one-game season. It's hard to be in desperation mode, but if you are in that mode, who knows," Pederson said. "I do know this: it's not about one guy; it's about eleven on offense, defense, and special teams. A lot of contributing factors go into winning a game."

The playoffs had arrived. The Eagles had two weeks to get ready for the first challenge.

CHAPTER FOURTEEN

THE UNDERDOGS

Pastor Ted Winsley had a purpose at the start of the playoffs when he began a special three-part series in his weekly Bible study with the Eagles. Three sermons because three games meant the Eagles would reach the Super Bowl.

"I put *Part 1 of 3* right there on the top of the notes," Winsley said with a smile.

Winsley called the lesson: "Faith to Subdue Your Dream." He taught from Hebrews 11. The first verse says: "Now faith is confidence in what we hope for and assurance about what we do not see." The chapter talks about the faith displayed by Abel, Enoch, Noah, Abraham, Sarah, Barak, Samson, Jephthah, David, and several others throughout the Old Testament.

"They subdued giants," Winsley said. "All of those people had one thing in common: none of them looked qualified to do what they did, and all of them had to use their faith to subdue their dream."

The Eagles didn't look qualified to win the Super Bowl, especially after losing Carson Wentz. They weren't even expected to get this far this season. Most of the analysts and experts predicted they'd be a fringe playoff team. The consensus was ten wins, at best. Many projections had the Eagles going 9–7, including mine. It was only Year 2 of the Wentz Era. He needed time to develop. He was expected to have more growing pains. Popular opinion was the Eagles were a year away from being a legitimate championship contender.

But Doug Pederson wasn't buying it. A week before training camp started, he boldly proclaimed his team "probably had more talent" than the powerhouse Green Bay Packers teams he played for in the mid-1990s. Pederson was the No. 3 quarterback behind Brett Favre and Jim McMahon in 1996 when the Packers beat New England in the Super Bowl. He was third-string behind Favre and Steve Bono the following season when Green Bay lost to Denver in its bid to repeat.

"There has to be a combination of blending all of this talent with a coaching staff, with my ideas and philosophy, to bring all that together, with the egos aside—put pride aside—and just go focus on winning [each] game that we have in front of us," Pederson said. "I'm a big believer that if you do that, then you look back at the end of the season, and you're probably going to be where you want to be, and that's playing in the postseason."

Pederson didn't want to put a limit on his team's expectations. He had confidence in them and wanted to send a message that anything short of winning a Super Bowl isn't good enough.

"If you win the Super Bowl, that's a successful year," he said. "Thirty-one teams failed to win the Super Bowl. I think if you're not winning or playing in that game, everyone's trying the next year. I think success can be measured in a few different [ways]. If we go 8–8, is that a successful year? I don't coach to be average. I'll tell you that. These players don't practice the way they do to be average. We're all in this together. We'll just continue to work every single day until we get to that goal."

His comments drew national headlines, of course. Fans thought Pederson was crazy to compare his team to the championship Packers teams in the 1990s. They hoped he was right, but too many people didn't even believe in Pederson as the coach going into his second season. But Pederson's point reached the players. Strive to be the best. Frank Reich reminded everyone going into the playoffs that Pederson predicted greatness for this team.

"Coach said at the beginning of the year that we were going to set out to do something special, and that's what we believe. That's what we believe we're in the process of doing," Reich said.

———————

Depending on the results of wild-card weekend, the Eagles would play either the New Orleans Saints, the Carolina Panthers, or the Atlanta Falcons in their first playoff game. Some coaches give their team a week off during the bye round. Pederson wanted them on the field, and players were eager to practice. They weren't happy with their performance in the final two games of the regular season, so they asked Pederson to increase the intensity at practice. Malcolm Jenkins and other members of the team's leadership council told Pederson in their weekly meeting they would like to put their pads on for one practice session in each of the next two weeks before the first game. Pederson happily obliged their request. He had held light walkthrough practice sessions late in the season to keep guys fresh.

"I listen to my guys, and I think they understand that there is a sense of physicality that we have to get back to," he said.

When the Eagles took the field for their normal Wednesday practice, it had the feel of training camp in August. Tackling wasn't allowed, and full contact was limited, but things got a little physical.

"You could hear the pads clacking," linebacker Nigel Bradham said. "We were really going after each other."

A few days later, the Eagles found out which team would be their first opponent. The Falcons beat the Rams 26–13 in an upset on the road to set up a divisional round game in Philadelphia. Atlanta was 10–6 in the regular season, one year after an epic collapse in the Super Bowl. The Falcons blew a 28–3 second-half lead against the Patriots and lost in overtime. They earned the final playoff berth in the NFC and were on a quest to atone for that devastating loss to the Patriots. Oddsmakers made them an historic 2½-point favorite. The Eagles were the first No. 1 seed to open the playoffs as an underdog since the NFL started awarding home-field advantage based on winning percentage.

The Falcons had impressive wins over the Saints and Panthers in December and had just defeated the Rams soundly. Quarterback Matt Ryan was the NFL's Most Valuable Player in 2016. Julio Jones is one of the best receivers in the game. Devonta Freeman and Tevin Coleman are a formidable running-back tandem. The defense was vastly improved. But installing the Falcons as favorites on the road in a hostile environment was an insult to the Eagles and their fans.

"We've been disrespected all year," Eagles cornerback Jalen Mills said. "We know how people view us, but we always find a way to win."

Players quickly got tired of hearing they were underdogs. Chris Long and Lane Johnson came up with an idea. They searched online for German Shepherd masks and bought a pair. Their plan was to wear them after winning the game to mock the people who labeled them underdogs.

All they had to do now was win.

———

The Falcons-Eagles matchup was the first game on the NFL's weekend schedule for the divisional round of the playoffs. It was 28 degrees and windy on a late Saturday afternoon in South Philadelphia. Lincoln Financial Field was loud and rowdy. Fans had been tailgating for hours, eagerly anticipating the Eagles' first playoff game in four years.

Atlanta won the coin toss but deferred to the second half, choosing to let Nick Foles and Philadelphia's offense get the ball first. Everyone was wondering which version of Foles would show up. Would it be the quarterback who performed so well in his first five quarters of action after replacing Carson Wentz? Or the guy who struggled so much in the next five quarters that some ill-advised folks questioned whether he would be benched?

Doug Pederson spent time during the bye week watching every snap Foles took during his sensational 2013 season. He made sure Foles also watched all the plays to see what made him excel. Pederson focused specifically on Foles' performance against the Saints in Philadelphia's wild-card playoff loss that season.

"I saw a guy that stood in there, took some shots in that game, delivered some great throws in that game, and led the team back to at least the go-ahead touchdown late in the game," Pederson said. "That's the type of quarterback that we have."

Pederson showed his confidence in Foles right away, calling

for a deep pass on the first play of the game. Foles slipped and underthrew Torrey Smith terribly. The ball fluttered in the wind, but Smith drew a pass interference penalty when he stopped running to come back for the short throw. It was a 42-yard gain and the Eagles already were in field-goal range at Atlanta's 33-yard line. But Jay Ajayi fumbled after running for 6 yards on the next play and the Falcons recovered.

Matt Ryan drove them to the Eagles 15 before the drive stalled and Matt Bryant kicked a 33-yard field goal to give Atlanta a 3–0 lead.

With Wentz standing on a crutch, watching from the sideline and offering his insight and encouragement, Foles found his rhythm on the offense's third possession. Pederson, a masterful play caller, surprised the defense with an inside counter to Nelson Agholor, who ran 21 yards to the Falcons 3. Pederson stayed aggressive, going for it on fourth down from the 1 instead of kicking a field goal. LeGarrette Blount ran in for the score, and the Eagles led 6–3. Jake Elliott missed the extra point, but made up for it by booting a 53-yard field goal as time expired at the end of the first half after Foles made a clutch throw to Alshon Jeffery to set it up. The Falcons led 10–9 at halftime, but Philadelphia's defense shut them down in the second half. Foles led the offense on two long drives that ended with Elliott kicking field goals. Then it came down to the defense.

Ryan directed the Falcons to the 9-yard line. They had a first down with 1:19 left in the game. Fans were on edge, standing and screaming for a stop.

Eagles defensive coordinator Jim Schwartz inherited one of the worst units in the NFL when he joined Pederson's staff in 2016 and quickly turned them into one of the league's best. The Eagles didn't allow any points in the final two minutes of any game during the regular season. Now they had to find a way to stay perfect with the season hanging in the balance.

Atlanta moved to the 2 in three plays. Fourth down. One more play. Instrumental music from *Rocky* blared from the stadium's sound system. Rocky Balboa, the fictional boxer played by Sylvester Stallone, has been a Philadelphia icon for decades. He was an underdog just like these Eagles.

The Falcons inexplicably ran a play that limited Ryan's options, a rollout that took half the field away from the quarterback. Ryan rolled to his right. Jones, the all-world receiver, was the intended target. Jalen Mills had one-on-one coverage. Jones slipped in the end zone, got up, and positioned himself behind Mills. Ryan was under pressure when he tossed the ball up in the corner of the right end zone. Mills and Jones both leaped. Jones has a three-inch height advantage. Fans held their breath. The ball sailed through Jones' hands and hit the ground. Incomplete. The Eagles began to celebrate and the crowd erupted in cheers, releasing all that nervous energy stored up for two weeks.

Final score: Eagles 15, Falcons 10.

Foles passed his biggest test yet. He completed 23 of 30 passes for 246 yards. He didn't have any touchdown passes but didn't commit any turnovers.

"I am very humbled to win this game and to be a part of this team," Foles said. "That's what it's always been about. I know there was a lot of people against us this last week, just answering questions and just hearing about it. But the biggest thing about this is that it's sports, that's part of it. The biggest thing in our locker room is we believe in one another. Everyone believes, and that was on display. The city of Philadelphia obviously believes because they were here and loud. So we are grateful for that. Honestly, it's unbelievable to win this game, and we are not finished."

The underdogs were moving on to the NFC championship game.

As the final seconds ticked off the clock, Lane Johnson went to the sideline and grabbed his German Shepherd mask from Jason Peters' coat pocket. He put it on his head and walked off the field barking.

"Everybody is calling us underdogs," Johnson said. "Anything we can use as extra motivation, we'll use. That's what makes the game fun."

Chris Long also wore his dog mask off the field and during parts of his interviews in the locker room. He planned to walk off the field with Johnson but didn't see him. "I couldn't find his scent," Long joked.

Writers whipped out their phones to take pictures and record video while television cameras locked in on Long and Johnson. Fans didn't need any convincing. Philadelphia has always been an underdog city, stuck between New York and Washington, D.C.

The rest of the team joined them in embracing the underdog role.

"Just keep on disrespecting us and we're going to keep proving people wrong," Alshon Jeffery said. "We just believe in one another; we don't care what anybody else says. We're just going to keep believing in one another and just keep fighting."

Johnson and Long didn't realize what they started was about to turn into a Philly phenomenon. Fans loved the masks and bought them up online. They were going to be allowed to wear them to the next game. Johnson created an "Underdogs" T-shirt with 65 percent—his uniform number is 65—going to fund Philadelphia schools. The NFL's official pro shop also jumped on the idea and produced a version of the T-shirt. Long, who donated his entire season's salary to fund education initiatives, made sure the league didn't profit off the shirts. He called them out in a post on social media. Johnson joined in.

Long tweeted: "Hey NFL you should donate the proceeds to charity like we did."

The league quickly announced 100 percent of the proceeds would also go to Philadelphia schools.

The Eagles were winning in everything.

SILENCING DOUBTERS

Nobody could have predicted Nick Foles and Case Keenum would be the starting quarterbacks in the NFC championship game. They took long, winding roads to get to this point. Foles began the season backing up Carson Wentz for the Eagles. Keenum was Sam Bradford's backup for the Minnesota Vikings. But the two quarterbacks had far more in common. They spent one year together with the St. Louis Rams in 2015 and formed a friendship, two brothers in Christ who put their faith first. Foles lost his starting job to Keenum late in that season with the Rams and joined the Kansas City Chiefs in 2016 after briefly contemplating retirement. The Vikings had considered acquiring Foles from the Chiefs after Teddy Bridgewater was injured in August 2016 but made a trade with the Eagles to get Bradford. Keenum played a second season with the Rams and helped prepare Jared Goff for the starting job. Both guys then joined their new teams as insurance policies until injuries forced them into the starting lineup.

Keenum had the best season of his career after Bradford hurt his knee in September. He led the Vikings to a 13–3 record and the No. 2 seed in the NFC. One day after the Eagles beat the Falcons, the Vikings needed a "Minneapolis Miracle" to advance. Down 24–23 to the New Orleans Saints, Keenum threw a 61-yard touchdown pass to Stefon Diggs on the final play to send the Vikings to the next round to face Philadelphia.

In a television interview on the field immediately after the game, Keenum said, "It's probably gonna go down as the third best moment of my life; behind giving my life to Jesus Christ, marrying my wife, and this one is right there close."

Plenty of people doubted Keenum throughout his career. Once he got a chance to prove himself, he took advantage of it. One guy who knew Keenum had the ability to succeed was his old buddy.

"Case's success and the way he plays doesn't surprise me because him and I were together and we prepared together," Foles said. "We were around each other every day. But I think the big message there is no matter what happens, you've just got to keep believing in yourself, keep working hard, and just never give up."

Keenum called Foles a "great guy" and said their wives are good friends.

"Great faith, great family, great football player," Keenum said. "Prepares well, extremely talented, big arm, and he's really, really athletic too. I know he has a lot of confidence, and I'm looking forward to playing against him."

Keenum vs. Foles in the NFC championship game—it seemed like a Disney script.

Once again, the Eagles were underdogs at home. Oddsmakers listed the Vikings as 3½-point favorites to win the NFC championship game in Philadelphia even though teams who played inside a dome were 0–12 in conference title games outdoors. But that's old history. The Vikings had the stingiest defense in the NFL and a solid quarterback with several weapons on offense, including receivers Stefon Diggs and Adam Thielen. They were one win away from becoming the first team to play a Super Bowl in its home stadium.

For the first time since the Eagles played at Los Angeles, weather conditions weren't much of a factor. The temperature was mild—47 degrees—at kickoff and the wind was calm at 5 miles per hour. The quarterbacks had no excuses to make poor throws.

Lincoln Financial Field was vibrating at kickoff. Fans were determined to make so much noise that Case Keenum and Minnesota's offense wouldn't be able to hear anything at the line of scrimmage. The Vikings got the ball first, and Keenum quickly moved them down the field. He found a weakness in Philadelphia's defense and tossed a 25-yard touchdown pass to Kyle Rudolph, quieting the raucous crowd. The Vikings were 7–0 when they scored first during the season so this was a good sign for them.

The Eagles knew they were in for a battle against a defense that allowed the fewest points—only 15.8 per game—and fewest yards. Nick Foles had to be at his best and the offense couldn't afford to make mistakes or miss opportunities. Right away, however, they missed one on the first possession. Foles threw a deep pass to Torrey Smith who had sped past a defender, but the ball hit his back shoulder and slipped through his hands.

Midway through the first quarter, Philadelphia's defense changed the momentum of the game. Chris Long swatted Keenum's left arm and chest, altering his throwing motion, and

Patrick Robinson intercepted the underthrown pass. Robinson wasn't content with the pick. He turned into a running back, zigzagged across the field, and pointed out a player so teammate Ronald Darby could throw a block to spring him into the end zone. His 50-yard touchdown return tied the game. Keenum was rattled. The crowd was in a frenzy.

Next time the Eagles had the ball on offense, Foles made one precision pass after another. LeGarrette Blount rumbled into the end zone from 11 yards out to give Philadelphia a 14–7 lead.

Late in the second quarter, the Vikings were driving for the tying score but the defense delivered again. Derek Barnett sacked Keenum, and Chris Long recovered the fumble. The turnover led to another big play for Philadelphia's offense. Foles, who isn't known for being elusive, escaped a sack and threw a 53-yard touchdown pass to Alshon Jeffery to extend the lead to 21–7. A field goal made it 24–7 at halftime, and fans were already starting to celebrate.

The Eagles received the kickoff to start the second half, and Doug Pederson maintained the aggressive approach that got them to this point. He called a flea flicker for the first time all season. The trick play worked perfectly. Foles handed the ball to Corey Clement and received the return pitch. He lofted a beautiful deep pass to Smith, who made an excellent over-the-shoulder catch for a 41-yard touchdown. Now fans were dancing in the stands and jumping on their phones to book their trips to Minnesota for the Super Bowl.

But Foles wasn't done yet. He tossed a 5-yard touchdown pass to Jeffery early in the fourth quarter. Wentz, who was walking with a cane now, flashed a big smile after the pass and gave Pederson a fist-bump. Actor Bradley Cooper, a longtime Eagles fan, pumped both of his fists from his seat in a suite. The rest of the fourth quarter had a party atmosphere and the defense continued to dominate. The underdog Eagles cruised to a 38–7 victory, setting up a rematch against the Patriots, Bill Belichick, and Tom Brady. The Patriots had defeated the Eagles 24–21 in the Super Bowl thirteen years earlier. It was time for revenge. No better way to win the franchise's first Super Bowl than to beat the greatest coach of all-time and the greatest quarterback.

Foles's final statistics were eye-popping. He completed 26 of 33 passes for 352 yards, three touchdowns, and no turnovers. Pederson sent backup Nate Sudfeld into the game to take the final snap and kneel so Foles could walk off the field and get a standing ovation from the fans. Foles waved both of his arms, soaking in the adoration of 69,596 fans in attendance. He got hugs and congratulations from everyone on the sideline. One of the first guys who came over to Foles was Wentz. Long, who played with Foles for one season in St. Louis, yelled, "I always believed in you." Pederson received a Gatorade bath from Malcolm Jenkins and Chris Maragos. Jeffrey Lurie danced awkwardly on the sideline. Fans cheered wildly. Players made "snow angels" with the green confetti on the field and the team celebrated its biggest win yet.

"All glory belongs to God," Foles said. "I'm just grateful and humbled to be a part of this team, to be in this moment, and to share it with our family, our fans, all of the people who love the Philadelphia Eagles, this franchise, and my teammates. It is honestly unbelievable, and words just can't describe it."

Pederson, a career backup quarterback turned coach, embraced Foles, a former backup turned superstar.

"I just told him how proud I am of him and I loved him," Pederson said. "Just so happy for him and what he's been through and everything now to finally put not only himself but help this football team get to where we want to go and hopefully finish the year right."

Despite losing Carson Wentz, the Eagles were going to the Super Bowl with a chance to bring home the Vince Lombardi Trophy for the first time in franchise history. But Goliath stood in their way. Belichick, Brady, and the Patriots were five-time champions looking to repeat.

"No one thought we were going to be here after Carson went down, but it's the resiliency of this team, how much we love playing for one another, and how much we love the game of football," Zach Ertz said.

The city of Philadelphia rallied around Foles, the backup quarterback who was one victory away from becoming a folk hero. Several billboards were posted throughout Philly and South Jersey that read, "From Wentz We Came; In Foles We Trust."

UNFINISHED BUSINESS

Jeffrey Luric was vindicated. The Eagles owner made two unpopular decisions when he put Howie Roseman back in charge of personnel and hired Doug Pederson to be the head coach.

Two years later, his team was heading to the Super Bowl thanks to the leadership and work of both men. Roseman assembled one of the league's top scouting departments led by Joe Douglas and found a way to build a team that was set up to win in the present and future. He drafted Carson Wentz. He brought Nick Foles back to Philly. He acquired Jay Ajayi and Ronald Darby in trades. He signed Alshon Jeffery, Torrey Smith, LeGarrette Blount, Chris Long, and Patrick Robinson in free agency. All of these guys played major roles throughout the season. Jeffery, Smith, Blount, and Robinson scored touchdowns in the NFC championship game. Those were just some of the moves Roseman made to reshape and rebuild the roster in only two years.

"I think, number one, he's a very, very smart guy," Lurie said of Roseman. "In the role today to be in charge of football operations, it is so much more than simply what has been in the past decades with scouting. Scouting is a big part of it, but you have to manage in so many ways short-term needs, mid-term needs, long-term needs. We found ourselves in an interesting situation where this is Year 2 of the plan, but we have a quarterback that was advancing by leaps and bounds and a team that was playing great, great defense, and an offensive line that was really good. We thought, 'You know, why can't we win it all?' We took an approach where we were going to do everything possible that could help our team this year, and at the same time not relinquish any options going forward. I think that was the key to the strategy. It took Howie and Joe Douglas and their staffs a lot of work to figure out going after [free agents] all over the roster. We were aggressive at the trade deadline because we thought we had a chance. Normally you wouldn't do that, but we thought we had a chance."

Roseman gave his boss credit for giving him the freedom to make bold moves.

"Jeffrey wants us to be aggressive and take risks," Roseman said. "He believes that if you don't take risks, you have no chance of being great—you're going to be in the middle. When you have an owner that says, 'Hey, don't be afraid to fail; go after what we believe in,' it's easier to take those risks."

Roseman had plenty of opportunities in the weeks before the Super Bowl to gloat about his success and how he overcame a one-year hiatus to become one of the league's most celebrated executives. But each time he insisted on taking the high road.

"I haven't thought a lot about it. I can honestly tell you that the greatest gift will be winning the world championship," Roseman said six days before the Eagles played against the Patriots.

"That will be for our organization, for our players, our coaches, and Philadelphia. This is a lot bigger for me. This is an opportunity to do something this organization, this team, has never done. When you think about that atmosphere and the opportunity we have, there's no way to think about anything else."

Enthusiastic Eagles fans went from vilifying Roseman to serenading him with chants of "Howie! Howie! Howie!" whenever they saw him in Minnesota. Instead of pointing fingers, pounding his chest, or blaming others for the humiliation he endured when Lurie banished him from football decisions and allowed former coach Chip Kelly to run the show in 2015, Roseman called that period "probably one of the best things to happen to me." He used that year to study the management styles of other executives in different sports and to learn more about the value of developing strong relationships at work.

"I felt like I had to look into myself and figure out a way to make people know I cared about them and make time for relationships," Roseman said. "Sometimes when you're in your job, when you're in a busy job, you kind of overlook some of those things, and I felt that that wasn't the right thing to do and how was I going to work on that, and I thought that was the most important thing because I care about a lot of people here. They're family to me. So for people not to know how you feel, whether that's your friends or your family, that's hurtful to me."

Roseman and Pederson have developed an excellent relationship built on trust and respect. They communicate multiple times each day and have been on the same page since the first day they began working together.

"I think when you talk about Doug's role, there's no decision that we make where he's not involved," Roseman said. "We never just say: 'Hey coach, here's a guy. He's on your team now.' We're really taking directives from him and his staff about what they're looking for in their players. It's not necessarily what I or Joe Douglas or anyone on our staff wants. It's what the coaches are looking for at each position, and we narrow it down to give them a small list of guys to look at. Doug and his whole staff are incredible people, incredible workers, and we're fortunate to have them."

Pederson put together a strong coaching staff with Frank Reich as the offensive coordinator and Jim Schwartz in charge of the defense. He changed the culture in the locker room, instilling core values of love, brotherhood, and unselfishness.

"I spent a lot of time with players at the end of that [2015] season and I thought what was really needed was a kind of leadership that leads with a genuineness, a real genuineness," Lurie said. "And people laughed when I used the term 'emotional intelligence,' but that's probably a really good way to describe it, and I think in sports today, there's many styles. There's a lot of great coaches. They all have their different styles, but the one common ground among them all is absolute consistency and genuineness. And Doug Pederson is just himself. And at times, that's very humble, and at times, it's just very real. At times, that's very bright. At times, it's tough. But he does it in a true, genuine way and I think players really respond to that in today's world."

Like Roseman, Pederson is too humble to boast. Carson Wentz said Pederson "has no ego." Pederson considers his "emotional intelligence" a byproduct of being a former player.

"I think that having the connection, having been in the locker room, having an understanding of the dynamic of what a team needs, what a team should feel, how we should practice, how we should play, when to take the pads off, when to put the pads back on, I think all of that is part of that emotional intelligence that I try to strive for and to have with the guys," Pederson said. "I think that relationship has gone a long way this season."

Lurie vowed to win multiple championships when he bought the Eagles for $195 million in 1994. He once called his franchise the NFL's "gold standard" during a state-of-the-team address. He was criticized for years for making that comment because the team hadn't won a Super Bowl title. Despite plenty of success throughout his tenure, they didn't win the Big One. The Eagles lost to Oakland in the Super Bowl after the 1980 season and lost to New England following the 2004 campaign in their only appearances in the first fifty-one Super Bowls. Ending the franchise's fifty-seven-year championship drought was everyone's goal.

"All of our focus, as it's been the whole year, is to win it all," Lurie said. "It's not to go to the Super Bowl. I think we're on a special trip to Minneapolis, and there is only one goal in mind. That's to win a world championship. That's what we're all obsessed with. This is the most passionate fan base in the NFL, if not in sports. They care so much, they're our partners, and we just want to win so badly for them."

Pederson echoed that feeling. Getting to the Super Bowl wasn't going to be good enough.

"There's a lot of unfinished business still to do," Pederson said. "There is one game left."

There was also still a sense of unfinished business left over from the last time the Eagles played the Patriots in the Super Bowl. That was supposed to be the year for Philadelphia. After Andy Reid's team lost the NFC championship game three straight years following the 2001–2003 seasons, Lurie gave the green light to do whatever it takes to get to the next level. The Eagles acquired superstar receiver Terrell Owens and signed star defensive end Jevon Kearse. Donovan McNabb had his best season in the NFL throwing to Owens and the offense was sensational. Kearse, Brian Dawkins, and Jeremiah Trotter led a dominant defense. The Eagles won their first seven games, finished 13–3, and beat Michael Vick and the Atlanta Falcons in the NFC championship without Owens, who was injured.

Owens made a remarkable return from ankle surgery and gave a heroic performance in the Super Bowl, but McNabb tossed three interceptions to go with three touchdown passes, and the Patriots won by a field goal.

The biggest difference between the 2004 Eagles and the 2017 Eagles was the unity and brotherhood on the team. It started at the quarterback position. McNabb had an excellent career and is a member of the team's Hall of Fame but he lacked the type of leadership skills Wentz and Foles bring to the team. McNabb was a sensitive guy, and always seemed concerned about fan and media criticism. He was known to have a passive-aggressive personality. Though he went to Bible study every week, McNabb appeared to have a tough time applying those lessons to his everyday life. Many believe his ego got in the way. Wentz and Foles are genuinely humble. That filters down to their teammates.

"We had a large number of believers on that team, but it wasn't a Christian culture," Pastor Ted Winsley said of the 2004 Eagles. "There wasn't the same connectivity and synergy among the team. This team, whether they are believers or not, they believe that those guys believe and they respect it, and even though it's not their thing, they believe it works."

CHAPTER SEVENTEEN

RESPECT, NOT FEAR

O ne guy wore a shark costume. Another wore a full football uniform. Someone else sported a dog mask. And those were members of the "media" with weird attire kicking off the wildest week in sports.

Welcome to Super Bowl Opening Night, the wacky spectacle held Monday evening before the Big Game. More than five thousand media people from all over the world filled a hockey arena in downtown St. Paul, Minnesota, eager to ask the New England Patriots and Philadelphia Eagles a litany of questions that are usually more inane than intelligent. A female reporter from Mexico once wore a wedding dress to the event and asked Tom Brady to marry her before the Patriots played the New York Giants in the 2008 Super Bowl. The two-week buildup for the championship game is one of the most overhyped periods on the sports calendar. Teams are fortunate they get to practice at home the first week before the media circus fully takes over.

"I've got to keep things on a rigid, tight schedule, and make sure the guys are focused on the job at hand," Doug Pederson said. "We've come this far and want to make sure that we stay focused. We have a great locker room. I trust my leaders to get the job done. I think the team that can put aside the distractions and focus on the game is going to be the team that's probably going to benefit from that."

The Eagles arrived in frigid Minnesota on Sunday, one week before the game and one day ahead of the Patriots who have plenty of experience dealing with the frenzy and try to avoid as much of it as they possibly can. It was the tenth Super Bowl appearance for the Patriots and eighth in seventeen seasons with Bill Belichick and Tom Brady. The four-time Super Bowl MVP got rock-star treatment, as usual, on the first night of media availability. Reporters with notepads, microphones, and cameras lined up twelve-deep in front of the podium where Brady spoke for forty-five minutes. The Patriots went first, and they were in an all-business mood. Belichick, known for wearing cut-off sleeveless sweatshirts and hoodies on the sideline, stepped up his wardrobe, wearing a dark navy suit, white shirt, and blue tie. Belichick even cracked a smile a few times but he mostly looked like someone who was about to have his wisdom teeth extracted. It's no secret Belichick does not enjoy talking to reporters, and Opening Night brings out the worst side.

After the Patriots finished their mandatory interview period, the Eagles walked out, and captains from both teams posed for a group photo. Both quarterbacks—Brady and Nick Foles—did a joint interview on stage in which they gave coaches and teammates credit and showed mutual respect.

Then it was time for the Eagles. Fans of the Patriots and Vikings lustily booed, but Eagles fans drowned it out with

"E-A-G-L-E-S!" chants. Pederson wore a gray team polo shirt, jeans, and a cap. He was loose, relaxed, and comfortable, setting the tone for his team to enjoy the week. The Eagles soaked in the experience—only seven players on Philadelphia's active roster had won a Super Bowl while thirty-two players on New England's roster had a combined sixty games of Super Bowl experience. Players walked around recording videos with their phones, answering outrageous questions from "journalists" dressed in clown outfits and more. Some players took turns holding the microphones and asking their teammates questions. Julie Ertz, a soccer star and wife of Zach Ertz, had fun interviewing some of her husband's teammates as one of several celebrity reporters on site.

Zach and Julie were a big story during the week. The couple were married on March 26, 2017 but they don't have a chance to spend much time together because of their schedules. Julie is a midfielder for the United States women's national soccer team and the Chicago Red Stars of the National Women's Soccer League. She was named the 2017 U.S. Soccer Female Player of the Year before the Eagles began their playoff run.

"Julie is the best athlete in the family," Zach Ertz said every time he was asked the question.

The Ertzes rely on their faith to maintain their strong relationship and overcome the difficulties of being apart so often.

"I got baptized the day before I got married because I wanted the world to know that I was dedicating my life to Christ," Zach Ertz said. "Julie and I have an amazing marriage right now, and hopefully we will be able to continue that. I see her four days out of a month, six days out of a month, especially [during soccer season] with her schedule and her being in Chicago and me being in Philly. There's just so much distance and, at times, temptation that can pull you away from each other, honestly. Our foundation in Christ is so important. I trust her relationship with Jesus, and she trusts me with Jesus. If we didn't have that relationship with Jesus, I would honestly say that our relationship would be impossible because we would be comparing our marriage with everyone else's around us, and there really isn't anyone with the same situation as us. There are people with similar situations but not the same sustained amount of time. The one thing since we've been married is we trust our relationship with the Lord. That's what's been the only thing we build our foundation on and the only thing we trust."

Julie made her rounds on Super Bowl Opening Night and even asked her hubby a few questions. "What's your favorite meal I make?" she asked. Zach's response: "She makes unbelievable tacos. She doesn't make them all the time, so I'm kind of upset about it, but when she does, they're off the chain."

One of the most important messages Pederson stressed to his team before they went to Minnesota was to avoid getting caught up in the mystique of the Patriots. Respect them and their accomplishments, but don't be in awe of them.

"That's a real issue that you have," Pederson said. "I think everybody in the league sort of envies their success to some extent, and rightfully so. They've been there, done that many times, and that's something that every other team would love to have. It's impressive, obviously, and it's well-respected and well-documented. At the same time, we're just going to prepare the same and try to block out all the noise. There's going to be a lot written to probably both extremes. But again, our guys have been resilient. They've been able to block that noise out. Once the ball is teed up and kicked off, just trust our players, trust our schemes, and play football."

Both teams were required to meet the media four straight

days from Monday through Thursday. Every storyline would be rehashed to the point it becomes intolerable to hear the same questions repeated every day. To their credit, players and coaches handled themselves with class. They understood intense scrutiny goes with having success.

Both teams didn't begin practicing until Wednesday, which is the typical regular-season schedule. Before taking the field for the first time at the indoor Gibson-Nagurski Complex on the campus of the University of Minnesota, the Eagles showed up that morning for their media session looking like a team that wasn't feeling any pressure. They were having a blast and had followed Pederson's advice intently so that they weren't intimidated by the Patriots. Jason Kelce donned his Elmer Fudd–style hat, a necessary item in the subzero temperatures in Minnesota. Fletcher Cox and Lane Johnson traded in their dog masks for wrestling masks. They wore Kelly green masks featuring an Eagles logo that resembled the ones World Wrestling Entertainment star Rey Mysterio and other *luchadores* wear in the ring.

"This was a gift from Mexico so I can have super powers all week," Cox joked. "I'm just having fun right now. We know why we're here. We can't come into this all uptight. You have fun when it's time to have fun and get serious when it's time to get serious. We talked to guys that have been around and been to Super Bowls before. They said that you can't go into this whole thing uptight. You still have to have fun."

Johnson had already adopted a wrestling star's persona in his interviews. He trash-talked Brady, calling him a "pretty boy."

"I definitely respect him and all that he's done in this league," Johnson said. "I'm not going to go into the Super Bowl worshiping this man and make him more than what he is."

Pederson installed the game plan a week earlier and worked the team hard in practice in Philadelphia. He wanted to hold lighter sessions without pads in the days leading up the game. The Eagles worked on fine-tuning details and refining plays. Pederson simulated the Super Bowl's thirty-minute halftime delay during the first practice, giving players a break so they would know what it would feel like and how to prepare for it on Sunday. Halftime during the regular season is twelve minutes. The team looked sloppy in practice after returning from the break, but Pederson wasn't concerned.

"We're so late in the season now, we know how to practice," he said. "Just making sure that we understand the importance. That's why I put us in that situation. Now we understand it. So it's a very teachable moment for our guys, our coaches for how to prepare for the second half of the football game."

Thursday's practice was more intense and had a faster pace. The Eagles worked on short-yardage, goal-line, and third-down situations during the one-hour, forty-five-minute session. They had a normal Friday practice the next day, emphasizing red-zone drills. On Saturday, Pederson had a surprise for his players. His good buddy, Hall of Famer Brett Favre, spoke to the players at the team hotel in the morning. Favre encouraged the Eagles to enjoy the moment and warned them not to become overconfident at any point in the game. He reminded them that the Patriots overcame a 28–3 deficit in the third quarter against the Atlanta Falcons in the Super Bowl a year earlier.

Favre's message was clear. It won't be easy to dethrone the defending champions. Bring your best effort.

SUPER SUNDAY

At last, the game had arrived. After all the hype and the hoopla, it was time for football. The New England Patriots against the underdog Philadelphia Eagles. New England was a 4½-point favorite, seeking its sixth Super Bowl victory, second in a row, and third in four years. The Eagles were going for their first championship since 1960. Beating Bill Belichick and Tom Brady would be a daunting task. Many analysts and experts picked the Patriots because of their experience. On my radio shows, I called the Eagles a better all-around team and said they would have the lead late in the fourth quarter and would need a strip-sack from someone like Chris Long or Brandon Graham to stop Brady, but I predicted it wouldn't happen and Brady would throw a touch-down pass to win it on the final drive.

Long-suffering Eagles fans had taken over Minnesota during the week. They were loud and proud at the Mall of America where the media headquarters were stationed. And they certainly made their presence felt hours before kickoff at U.S. Bank Stadium after braving the cold weather outside. On Sunday morning, the temperature in Minneapolis was minus-6 degrees, with a wind-chill factor of minus-25. Inside the domed stadium, it was cozy and comfortable. "E-A-G-L-E-S!" chants were almost non-stop, echoing throughout the building. Many fans brought their dog masks and barked between chants. They carried the dream of their fathers and grandfathers to see their beloved Eagles finally win a championship.

Malcolm Jenkins gathered the team for one more pep talk before their biggest game. "You wanna be world champs? You wanna be world champs? All it takes is for you to give everything you got for sixty minutes. That's all that stands between you and immortality. We've been the best team in this league from start to finish. They're just finding out, so show the world today."

The Eagles wore their green jerseys with white pants. The Patriots wore white jerseys and navy-blue pants. Carson Wentz, wearing his number 11 jersey and walking without a crutch or cane, hugged Nick Foles on the sideline and tapped him on the top of his helmet with both hands. "You're made for this. Enjoy it," Wentz told his friend.

New England won the coin toss but deferred to the second half. Starting from the 26-yard line, Foles came out firing. He completed three straight passes for a total of 23 yards. A 15-yard pass to Torrey Smith on third-and-12 extended the drive and a 16-yard pass to Corey Clement put the ball at the Patriots 5. But the Eagles couldn't score a touchdown and settled for Jake Elliott's 25-yard field goal. Teams know they can't miss opportunities against the Patriots, and this was a chance to jump ahead 7–0 instead of 3–0. Still, it was important for the Eagles to start strong.

Brady quickly connected on three passes for a gain of 47 yards, and the Patriots reached the Eagles 8 before their drive stalled.

Two-time All-Pro kicker Stephen Gostkowski made a 26-yard field goal to tie it at 3–3.

The Eagles only needed three plays on their next possession to show everyone they were going to make it a tough day for the Patriots. LeGarrette Blount busted loose for a 36-yard run against his former teammates, and Foles threw a 37-yard touchdown pass to Alshon Jeffery in the back of the end zone. Jeffery made a leaping catch over cornerback Eric Rowe, a former Eagle who started instead of Malcolm Butler. Belichick never explained his odd decision to bench Butler, who wasn't injured and had started every game the previous three seasons. Elliott missed the extra point and the Eagles led 9–3. They could only hope that missed point wouldn't be a factor at the end.

Foles encouraged the young kicker on the sideline. "We'll get you a bunch of opportunities," he told him.

Brady told his teammates in the huddle, "It's gonna be a dog-fight, boys."

Brady was ready for it. He escaped a sack on third-and-7 and threw deep to Danny Amendola for a 50-yard gain but the Patriots again had to settle for a field goal after they reached the Eagles' 8. This time, the snap was botched, and Gostkowski hit the left upright on a 26-yard attempt.

After the Eagles went three-and-out and punted for the only time in the game, Brady threw a 23-yard pass to Brandin Cooks on New England's first play but Jenkins crushed the speedy receiver with a devastating hit that knocked him out of the game with a concussion. Cooks had sixty-five catches for 1,082 yards and seven touchdowns during the season. His absence cost New England its primary deep threat.

"He's one of our best players so anytime you lose a great player, it's tough. Frustrating to lose him, but that's football," Brady said afterward.

Two plays after Cooks went down, the Patriots tried to trick Philadelphia's defense. Amendola took a handoff from James White on an end around and threw a pass to Brady, who was wide open running down the right side. Brady, who at forty years, one hundred eighty-five days old was the oldest non-kicker to appear in the Super Bowl, is one of the slowest quarterbacks in the league, but that play worked the last time New England tried it, ironically, against the Eagles in December 2015. Brady caught a pass and rumbled for 36 yards in that game. His only other career catch came in 2001 in his second season in the NFL. This was a strange time to try it on third down. Amendola's pass was on target, but the ball bounced off Brady's fingertips as he tried to make an over-the-shoulder grab. Flustered by the drop, the Patriots went for it on fourth-and-5 from Philadelphia's 35 and Brady's pass fell incomplete.

The Eagles took advantage of solid field position. Foles threw a 17-yard pass over the middle to Ertz on third down. He tossed a beautiful 22-yard pass down the right side over two defenders to Jeffery, who made the over-the-shoulder catch Brady couldn't make. Blount ran into the end zone from the 21 on the next play, giving the Eagles a 15–3 lead midway through the second quarter—they failed on a 2-point conversion.

"Fly! Eagles! Fly!" reverberated throughout the stadium, but it was way too early to celebrate and Eagles fans knew that.

Rex Burkhead turned a short pass into a 46-yard gain on New England's next play, but Brady again couldn't get the offense in the end zone. Gostkowski hit a 45-yard field goal to cut the deficit to 15–6. The Eagles then made their first mistake. Foles threw a deep pass to Jeffery that bounced out of his hands and was intercepted by Duron Harmon at the Patriots 2. It was the lucky break New England needed.

Wentz walked over to encourage Foles on the sideline: "Keep giving him a chance. He had that." Foles was unflappable: "We good. We good."

The turnover sparked the Patriots and Brady drove them 90 yards. A 43-yard pass to Chris Hogan set up James White's 26-yard touchdown run. Suddenly, it was 15–12. Gostkowski missed the extra point and two minutes remained in the first half.

New England was set to receive the kickoff to start the third quarter so the Eagles had an important possession. They couldn't give the ball right back to Brady. He was moving at will against their defense, and they were fortunate to only have allowed 12 points at that point. The offense had to take a lead into the locker room after controlling the game much of the first half. Foles came through with another clutch third-down play, tossing a 55-yard catch-and-run pass to Corey Clement to put the ball at the Patriots 8. Clement ran twice to get it to the 1 and an incomplete pass set up a tough decision with 38 seconds remaining in the half. A short field goal would give the Eagles an 18–12 lead. Failure to convert on fourth down would shift momentum to the Patriots.

Doug Pederson didn't hesitate. "I'm going for it right here," he yelled into his headset. The announcers calling the game on television and radio questioned his decision. Patriots players were surprised. But anyone who followed the Eagles closely since Pederson took over as the head coach wasn't surprised. He's always been aggressive. That was his style. He wasn't going to change his philosophy in the Super Bowl. Pederson called a time-out to make sure he would get the perfect play called. Foles walked over to his coach and suggested a play. "You want Philly Philly?" he said. Pederson looked up from his play chart, took a second to process the magnitude of the play and what his quarterback wanted to do. He shook his head confidently and said: "Yeah, let's do it."

"It shows a lot about Doug and how he trusts his players," Foles said. "You got to see a little insight into our relationship. There's a lot of trust, a lot of faith."

Foles walked into the huddle and relayed the play: "Here we go. Philly Special. Philly Special." Foles lined up in shotgun formation and motioned with his right hand for Clement to move behind him. Foles then walked up to the line of scrimmage and screamed: "Kill. Kill." He was trying to make the defense think he was changing the play and needed to get close enough for the linemen to hear him because of the crowd noise. Clement played along, gesturing with his right hand as if he didn't understand what was happening. Foles shuffled two steps to his right toward Lane Johnson and yelled: "Lane. Lane." That was the signal to snap the ball. Jason Kelce's snap went directly to Clement, who took the ball and started running toward his left. He tossed it nonchalantly in the air to Trey Burton coming around the end. Meanwhile, Foles slipped out to the right and ran a route into the corner of the end zone. Burton, a former quarterback in high school, caught the ball from Clement, switched it into his right hand, rolled to his right, and tossed a perfect pass to Foles standing all alone. Foles caught the ball for a touchdown. Everyone in the stadium and watching on television was stunned. It was a gutsy call executed to perfection.

On the local radio broadcast, Merrill Reese, the Eagles play-by-play announcer since 1977, said: "That's unbelievable." On the television broadcast, NBC analyst Cris Collinsworth said:

"This play call has a chance to be remembered as one of the all-time greats." Kevin Harlan, play-by-play announcer for Westwood One, said: "Holy smokes! What did we just see?"

Foles hugged Pederson on the sideline and told him: "I was feeling it."

The Eagles had been working on the play for a month after assistant coach Press Taylor suggested it during the playoff bye week. Taylor saw the Chicago Bears do it against the Minnesota Vikings in 2016. Pederson loved it but didn't get a chance to use it against the Falcons or Vikings. The team practiced it one last time during a walk through in the ballroom of their hotel a couple days before the Super Bowl. Burton had an option to run or throw to Foles. The Patriots were chasing Burton so he had no chance to run, but nobody covered Foles.

"When I heard Foles call 'Philly Special' in the huddle, I looked up wide-eyed," said Burton, who completed 11 of 17 passes in college. "The rest is history."

Instantly, the "Philly Special" became a legendary play, one the Eagles will never forget. One fan had Burton draw the play design on his arm along with his initials before a tattoo artist inked it for him.

The Eagles took a 22–12 lead into the locker room at halftime, but there was still a full half to play, and the Patriots are known for coming back. No lead is safe against Brady. He's engineered eleven fourth-quarter comebacks in the playoffs, including five in the Super Bowl. Everyone remembered what happened to the Falcons a year earlier. Eagles fans were too smart to start celebrating. They were optimistic with thirty minutes of football left to play, but they had grown accustomed to heartbreak after decades of failure.

After Justin Timberlake entertained the crowd with a half-time performance that featured some of his greatest hits and a tribute to Prince, Brady was ready to roll. All-Pro tight end Rob Gronkowski was unstoppable on the opening drive. He caught four passes for 68 yards, including a 5-yard touchdown pass.

But the Eagles answered on the next drive. Foles threw a 22-yard touchdown pass to Clement between two defenders. Clement made an excellent catch, maintaining control of the ball before he stepped out of the end zone. A video review upheld the call on the field, and the Eagles reclaimed their 10-point lead at 29–19. Brady came back with a 26-yard touchdown pass to Hogan as the offenses went back and forth. Neither defense could do anything.

Elliott kicked a 42-yard field goal on the second play of the fourth quarter to extend Philadelphia's lead to 32–26.

Now the Patriots got the ball following a touchback with a chance to take their first lead after trailing the entire game. They caught Philadelphia's defense off-balance by having Burkhead run three straight plays for a total 18 yards. Brady then threw four consecutive completions to get inside the red zone. On second down, Gronkowski made a leaping catch for a 4-yard touchdown, and Gostkowski kicked the extra point. New England led 33–32 with 9:22 remaining in the game. Patriots fans roared. Eagles fans fell silent. Missed opportunities, missed extra point, failed 2-point conversion. It had caught up to Philadelphia.

But the players were confident. Ertz said to Foles, "They can't stop us." Foles replied, "No, they can't." They were right. On the ensuing drive, Pederson had another tough decision. The Eagles faced fourth-and-1 from their 45. There was enough time, over five minutes, to punt the ball and hope for the defense to make a stop. But the defense hadn't really stopped Brady all day, and Pederson had confidence in his offense. He stayed aggressive.

Foles took the snap, eluded a sack and tossed a 2-yard pass to Ertz that was just enough to keep the drive going. Three straight passes to Nelson Agholor gained 38 yards. The Eagles were not only moving the ball but using up the clock. On third-and-7 from the 11, Foles fired a pass to Ertz over the middle. Ertz caught it in stride, ran a few steps and reached for the end zone. The ball bounced off the ground and back into his arms for a go-ahead touchdown. Pending review, of course. In a season when the NFL's catch rule was heavily criticized, it was fitting the final game could be decided by a controversial call. Referee Gene Steratore conferred with the replay officials, and it was confirmed that Ertz established himself as a runner after the catch so it was a touchdown once he crossed the goal line.

"One of my favorite moments during the game was everything going on during the review," Ertz recalled. "It was me and Trey Burton standing on the field literally just having a conversation 'They better not overturn this. If they overturn this the whole city is going to burn down.' There was so much going on around us, and Trey and I are just having a regular conversation. That's something I will always remember from that game."

Foles's pass to Clement for the 2-point conversion failed and the Eagles led 39–33 with 2:21 left. That was plenty of time for Brady to lead another one of his magical comebacks. Jenkins walked up and down the sideline, imploring the defense to "make a stop." Foles looked at Long and repeated, "Strip him. Strip him." Brady completed an 8-yard pass to Gronkowski to start the drive. Anxiety filled Eagles fans. Patriots fans have seen this before. The world has seen this before. The defense desperately needed to find a way to stop Brady. On second down, Brandon Graham, the longest-tenured player on Philadelphia's defense, burst through the line, hit Brady, and knocked the ball loose with his left hand. Derek Barnett scooped it up, and the Eagles had the ball. Players, coaches and everyone on the team's sideline rejoiced. Guys raised their arms triumphantly, jumped up and down, and began to celebrate. Still, it wasn't over.

There was 2:09 left in the game, and the Patriots had one time-out remaining plus the two-minute warning. Foles calmly looked at the guys in the huddle and said, "I love you guys, first off. Second, let's blow them off the ball, get a first down, and finish the thing."

They couldn't. Blount ran three times for only 4 yards. But Elliott delivered in the clutch. He nailed a 46-yard field goal to extend the lead to 41–33. The Patriots now had to score a touchdown and get the 2-point conversion to send the game to overtime. Only 58 seconds remained, and they had to drive 91 yards. Brady moved the Patriots to midfield for one more play. He took a deep drop, escaped Graham's grasp, and heaved a "Hail Mary" as Fletcher Cox knocked him to the ground. The pass headed toward Gronkowski, who was surrounded by several Eagles. Gronkowski leaped, and the ball hit his arms, bounced off a few other hands, and fell harmlessly to the ground.

Reese exclaimed on the radio broadcast: "The game is over! The Philadelphia Eagles are Super Bowl champions. Eagles fans everywhere, this is for you. Let the celebration begin!"

The Philadelphia Eagles had finally won their first Super Bowl title, beating the mighty New England Patriots in a scintillating game that featured several broken records, including most total yards (1,151) in any game in NFL history. It was the most action-packed, exciting championship game many people had ever witnessed.

The Eagles really did it. They won it all. I couldn't believe it. But I watched the scene unfold from my spot in the press box— row one, seat two—with no emotion. I gave up being a fan in 2000 when I interviewed for The Associated Press' Philadelphia sports writer's position. My former boss, Terry Taylor, made it clear credible journalists have no rooting interest so I stopped cold-turkey and haven't looked back. I never wanted to let her down and I have too much respect for the profession. But I couldn't help wonder how the young me would've reacted. I remember crying when the Eagles lost the Fog Bowl against the Chicago Bears in 1988. I was one of those long-suffering fans who bled green for the first 20-plus years of my life. This was a moment I longed to witness as a kid. Now it happened and I was stoic, completely focused on writing my story and recording a post-game podcast. I looked around and felt the euphoria in the stands.

"E-A-G-L-E-S!" chants rocked the stadium. In Philadelphia, thousands of fans piled into the streets to celebrate together. They climbed greased-up light poles, trash trucks, and awnings, sprayed beer, sang, chanted, and danced all night long.

On the field, after exchanging hugs and handshakes, players gathered in a circle, took a knee, held hands, and gave thanks to the Lord as Stefen Wisniewski led a passionate prayer. In their moment of greatest triumph, these brothers in Christ stopped to glorify God because that's what they always do and that's who they are.

I was in the locker room when the celebration continued, and the players once again came together for prayer, this time it was the entire team taking a knee to recite "The Lord's Prayer" upon Pederson's instruction.

Moments earlier, Pederson stood on stage with the Vince Lombardi Trophy sitting on a stand in front of him and was asked by NBC broadcaster Dan Patrick to explain how he went from coaching high school to winning a Super Bowl in nine years. "I can only give the praise to my Lord and Savior Jesus Christ for giving me this opportunity," Pederson said.

Foles was named MVP of the Super Bowl after leading the improbable victory. He completed 28 of 43 passes for 379 yards and three touchdowns and also became the first player ever to catch and throw a touchdown in the Super Bowl.

"Unbelievable. All glory to God," Foles said on stage while holding his seven-month-old daughter, Lily, who wore pink head-phones to protect her ears from the noise.

Then it was Ertz's turn on stage: "Glory to God, first and foremost. We wouldn't be here without Him."

Ertz later explained the importance of praising God on that platform. "Looking back on the past twenty-seven years of my life, there have been so many things that He has allowed me to overcome that I didn't even see Him working. He's put people in my life like Kyle [Horner], my mentors that have built me up to be ready when I'm on that stage. I felt a responsibility because of the platform that He has given us to give Him the praise and thanks for all He has done."

Hearing their coach glorify the Lord touched many players who weren't aware of Pederson's deep faith. Wentz is close with Pederson, and he knew he was a fellow believer because he would sometimes knock on his office door at 5:30 in the morning and interrupt his prayer and devotional time. Ertz heard that Pederson praised Jesus on stage after he was on the bus leaving the stadium and saw the comment circulating on social media.

"We never really heard him talk like that and that was almost like a green light, saying, 'I'm giving you the okay to do what you're doing,' and it had a profound impact on all of us because we play a sport where obviously some people are gonna be offended, but for our head coach to thank Jesus on that stage, it said to us, 'You guys are good to do what you're doing because I'm right there with you.' It was powerful."

The Eagles began the day worshiping Christ in a meeting room at the team hotel, and they finished it in worship on the field after their greatest professional victory.

CHAPTER NINETEEN

PARADE OF CHAMPIONS

They started gathering twelve hours early in freezing cold weather to make sure they could get a prime view of their heroes traveling along the parade route. They came by cars, buses, trains, and planes, and some even walked across a bridge from New Jersey to avoid traffic. They rented hotel rooms to watch from windows, they sat perched in trees, and they stood on rooftops, including a minister and about fourteen of his friends who caught a glimpse from the top of a church. They were huddled along sidewalks, packed up against police barricades, and they couldn't be happier.

Their beloved Eagles won their first Super Bowl four days earlier. It was time to celebrate a victory many people waited a lifetime to see. It didn't matter how cold, how crowded, how crazy it was going to be. Fans young and old flooded the streets, waved their flags and pennants, danced, sang, and partied like never before. Oh, they mixed in a few alcoholic beverages along the way.

Several people even scattered the ashes of deceased loved ones who didn't get to watch their favorite team finally win it all. Some said they were now ready to die in peace because they finally witnessed the Eagles earn the ultimate win in professional team sports.

The city held massive championship parades for the Phillies in 2008 and 1980, the 76ers in 1983, and the Flyers in 1974 and 1975. But football is king in Philadelphia, and fans had been waiting since 1960 for the Eagles to win it all. Schools, museums, courts, government offices, and even the Philadelphia Zoo were shut down to give people an opportunity to enjoy the festivities.

Led by a police escort, the Eagles departed from a parking lot near their stadium and began cruising down Broad Street in giant green buses adorned with "World Champions" signs. Before long, some of the guys, including Howie Roseman, Doug Pederson, and several players got off the bus to walk along the street, shake hands with fans, take selfies, and exchange high-fives and hugs. Pederson clutched the Vince Lombardi trophy and held it up high for everyone to see, even those who were twenty-rows deep in the crowd. Malcolm Jenkins sprayed champagne into the crowd. Jason Kelce wore a Mummers costume, a colorful green-and-pink sequined outfit he borrowed from a member of the Avalon String Band that marches in the traditional New Year's Day parade. Kelce used a policeman's bicycle and rode around the streets, sang a catchy new song he learned, and chugged a beer while preparing to deliver a speech nobody will soon forget.

It took the buses a few hours to eventually make their way to City Hall after the five-mile journey. Players, coaches and front-office staff had a chance to speak to the fans from the steps of the Philadelphia Art Museum—the ones that Sylvester Stallone famously climbed in *Rocky*.

Jeffrey Lurie addressed the crowd first. He thanked the fans, called the players "the most impressive group of men" he's ever been around and praised the coaches and staff.

"When you treasure selflessness, compassion, teamwork, trust in and love each other, and [have] incredible resilience through all the adversity and combine it with great focus and strategy, you become a world championship family," Lurie said. "We are just beginning."

Pederson was next. He had a similar message.

"We're not done yet. We have more to go, more to prove," Pederson declared. "This is our new norm."

Roseman followed.

"Philly, is this what heaven is like?" he exclaimed. "The best city in the world, the best fans in the world, and now we have the world championship. Get used to it."

Nick Foles was the first player to stand at the podium, overlooking a sea of green jerseys and confetti littering the Benjamin Franklin Parkway.

"I don't think words can really describe what is going on today," Foles said. "I have never seen so many people celebrating in unity one thing. It is an honor for us to bring y'all the Super Bowl. We finally did it. We're Super Bowl champs."

Chris Long and Lane Johnson led an "E-A-G-L-E-S" chant and barked like "underdogs." Brandon Graham talked about how the team embodied the attitude of the City of Brotherly Love. Carson Wentz told fans it was "a joy" to play in front of them. After Mack Hollins did the "Backpack Kid" dance, Kelce stole the show with an emotional speech that highlighted many of the criticisms that were directed at the team.

"I'm gonna take a second to talk to you about underdogs,"

Kelce said. "Howie Roseman, a few years ago, was relinquished of all control pretty much in this organization. He was put in the side of the building where I didn't see him for over a year. Two years ago, when they made a decision, he came out of there a different man. He came out of there with a purpose and a drive to make this possible. And I saw a different Howie Roseman. An underdog. Doug Pederson. When Doug Pederson was hired, he was rated as the worst coaching hire by a lot of freakin' analysts out there in the media. This past offseason, some clown named Mike Lombardi [a former NFL general manager] told him he was the least-qualified head coach in the NFL. You saw a driven Doug Pederson, a man who went for it on fourth down, went for it on fourth down, in the Super Bowl, with a trick play. He wasn't playing just to go mediocre. He's playing for a Super Bowl. And it don't stop with him. It does not stop with him.

"Jason Peters was told he was too old, didn't have it anymore. Before he got hurt, he was the best freaking tackle in the NFL. Big V [Halapoulivaati Vaitai] was told he didn't have it. Stefen Wisniewski ain't good enough. Jason Kelce is too small. Lane Johnson can't lay off the juice. Brandon Brooks has anxiety. Carson Wentz didn't go to a Division I school. Nick Foles don't got it. Corey Clement's too slow. LeGarrette Blount ain't got it anymore. Jay Ajayi can't stay healthy. Torrey Smith can't catch. Nelson Agholor can't catch. Zach Ertz can't block. Brent Celek's too old. Brandon Graham was drafted too high. Vinny Curry ain't got it. Beau Allen can't fit the scheme. Mychal Kendricks can't fit the scheme. Nigel Bradham can't catch. Jalen Mills can't cover. Patrick Robinson can't cover.

"It's the whole team. It's the whole team. This entire organization, with a bunch of driven men who accomplished something.

We were a bunch of underdogs. And you know what an underdog is? It's a hungry dog. And Jeff Stoutland has had this in our building for five years—it's a quote in the O-line room that has stood on the wall for the last five years: 'Hungry dogs run faster.' And that's this team. Bottom line is, we wanted it more. All the players. All the coaches. The front office. Jeffrey Lurie. Everybody wanted it more. And that's why we're up here today. And that's why we're the first team in Eagles history to hold that freakin' trophy."

Kelce concluded his five-minute speech with the expletive-filled "No One Likes Us, We Don't Care" song he learned earlier in the day. The crowd erupted in cheers while his teammates looked on with expressions ranging from disbelief to elation because he said what they felt but wouldn't dare express. Kelce became an instant legend in Philadelphia. His speech will forever be etched in the minds of everyone who heard it. It's classic Philadelphia, epitomizes the gritty, blue-collar mentality of the city and its fans. Many considered Kelce's speech an angry, emotional rant. But Eagles chaplain Pastor Ted Winsley saw a man who was affected by the Christian culture on the team.

"They called it a rant. I say it was a man who was impacted by God moving through believers," Winsley said. "He was impacted. Listen to it from the perspective of a guy who was moved to believe by the faith of the believers."

Winsley hopes to see Kelce in Bible study in the near future.

"We're gonna get him," Winsley said with confidence and a smile. "We're gonna put together a hit list of guys we're going to pray for and believe God will strategically save their lives."

There was no official estimate from the city on the size of the crowd, though officials believed it was the biggest crowd ever assembled for an event in Philadelphia. Many people disputed a report from a firm in Great Britain that estimated the size, based on pictures, at 700,000. If the team delivers on its promise, they'll get to do it again soon.

Four months later, the Eagles were scheduled to visit the White House for a traditional championship celebration. But President Donald Trump canceled the ceremony one day before the trip, citing players protesting during the national anthem. None of the Eagles took a knee during the "Star-Spangled Banner" throughout the 2017 season. Still, Trump said in a statement that some members of the Super Bowl championship team "disagree with their President because he insists that they proudly stand for the National Anthem, hand on heart, in honor of the great men and women of our military and the people of our country." I reported that only two players planned to make the trip to the White House along with Coach Doug Pederson and other members of the organization. Malcolm Jenkins and other players defended their stance, and emphasized the protests were not against the anthem, the country, the flag, or the military. Colin Kaepernick began the protests in 2016 over racial injustices. Jenkins and several others supported the important cause.

Instead of honoring the Eagles, Trump held a brief "Celebration of America" on the White House lawn. The Eagles refused to engage in a back-and-forth with the President and only issued the following statement: "We are truly grateful for all of the support we have received and we are looking forward to continuing our preparations for the 2018 season."

The team held an optional practice on the day it was supposed to be in the nation's capital and players showed their unity. When a cable news organization posted photos of Eagles players kneeling in prayer during a report on the White House fiasco—a gross misrepresentation of the facts—Zach Ertz spoke out. Teammates, fans and media supported him and an apology was issued. The next day, surrounded by cameras and microphones in front of his locker, Ertz demonstrated a forgiving heart.

"I wasn't mad, I wasn't upset, I think it was just kind of disappointed," Ertz said. "I'm not going to judge who created the video and I don't know what they're going through as an individual, what the network wanted them to do. I'm not here to judge anyone. I was disappointed a little bit, obviously, but at the same time, I'm not there to judge them. I just go about my day. I think that was kind of sad.

"I was most disappointed about, I feel like our community right now, there's either one side or the other. Whereas in my opinion, everyone should be trying to build up this country, build up everyone. No one should be trying to prove, beat down their point. It's not my job to beat down my opinion over someone else or vice versa. That's all I was kind of disappointed about."

CHAPTER TWENTY

NO QB CONTROVERSY

Nick Foles made it clear when he first replaced Carson Wentz, and he reiterated it after leading the Eagles to a Super Bowl victory: "It's Carson's team." There's no quarterback controversy in Philadelphia. The Super Bowl MVP knows he's going back to the bench once Wentz is ready to return from knee surgery. And, he's fine with it.

"My role is to help this team in practice while Carson's getting healthy, which I'm excited for," Foles said. "I want him to get back out there and get healthy and get back to [being] Carson Wentz. I want him to pick up off where he left off. That excites me from a friend's perspective and a teammate's perspective."

The biggest question after the Super Bowl was whether the Eagles would trade Foles to a team looking for a starting quarterback. His value skyrocketed after his spectacular performance in the playoffs. But Philadelphia's asking price was too high for several teams that opted to pursue other quarterbacks in free agency, trades, and the draft.

"It had to be the right deal for us to do that," Doug Pederson said. "I'm excited to have him. I'm ecstatic. It's a great quarterback room, great dynamic, and I'm excited that we still have all three guys."

Howie Roseman said the team feels "very good about the most important position in sports."

Sure, Foles wants to be a starter again. He certainly proved he's capable. He watched Kirk Cousins, Alex Smith, Sam Bradford, Case Keenum, and Tyrod Taylor change teams in the offseason. Instead of a new uniform and a starting job, Foles got a restructured contract. It included a $2 million raise for 2018, a chance to earn up to $23 million based on playing incentives, and a mutual option for 2019. Demanding a trade never entered Foles's mind. It's not his style, not the person he is.

"I always believed your actions speak louder than words. The key is to go out and lead your team and show people," Foles said. "There's definitely times where I'm tempted to look at the future, like any of us are. I'd be lying if that wasn't the case. But you have to reel back in and stay in the present because that doesn't do you any benefit. It's not easy because part of you wants to lead a team. I've been blessed to experience so much in my career so whenever those thoughts hit you, you take what I learned earlier in my career and say this is a really great spot and enjoy the moment. This is a special town. There's so much here I really enjoy. I've seen both sides of it. The grass isn't always greener on the other side. Do I want an opportunity to lead a team again? Absolutely. But am I trying to run away and do it right now? I'm grateful to be here."

Foles and his family are comfortable in Philadelphia. They have great friends, a strong Christian environment surrounding them, and his relationship with Wentz is special. It's rare to see such a bond between a starting quarterback and his backup, especially in these circumstances. But it's not surprising in this case because of who they are as men, as brothers in Christ. Wentz, Foles, and No. 3 quarterback Nate Sudfeld are very tight.

"Nate, Carson, and I have such a great group," Foles said. "It's a lot of fun to go to work, a great room to work in. We all understand our roles, and we all want the best for each other."

Wentz described his relationship with Foles as "pretty special."

"We've become so close ever since he first got here, developed a real friendship, a real relationship, more than just a working relationship, a true friendship between me and him—and Nate as well," Wentz said.

Wentz admitted it was tough for him to watch someone else lead his team to a Super Bowl victory. Still, he stayed out of the spotlight and allowed Foles to step up and be the man. Wentz was there in the meeting rooms every day during the week and on the sideline cheering during the playoff games. He gave Foles advice, helped him break down defenses, and did whatever he could to lend support.

"One of the greatest things about a person is when you see him celebrating somebody else's success," Frank Reich said. "To be happy for Nick who is at your position, that's the pretty cool thing about it. Of all the great things that he's done, it even more exemplifies the kind of leader that he is."

Wentz relied on his faith to get him through moments of self-pity after he was injured. It would've been easy for him to be angry at God, to question God's timing, to become bitter.

"It was a chance to practice what I preach and that I play for an audience of one, and it's not for myself," Wentz said. "God closed the door on the season for me, but I know He's going to open many other doors, and He's going to use me. It's human nature to want to be on that podium and be that guy. You grew up wanting to do that as a kid. To not be able to be up there, I wouldn't rather have anyone else up there other than Nick. It's really a special bond that we share, so I was challenged to look and say, 'Alright Nick, it's yours.' I wouldn't have rather passed it off to anybody else knowing his faithfulness in Christ and that he was ready for that. To see his story unfold as a friend and brother in Christ, for Jesus to get the glory through Nick and for Nick to reach more people because of it, I couldn't have asked for a better way given the circumstances."

Keeping Foles on the roster is an ideal scenario for Pederson in case Wentz gets injured again. Pederson recognizes it's a unique situation having a Super Bowl MVP return to a backup role without complaining. He's fortunate that man is Foles.

"He's totally fine being that mentor, sort of in that backup role, helping Carson along the way," Pederson said. "That's who Nick is. That's who he is. And when called upon, he's going to perform, but he understands this is Carson's team, and he's going to support him every way he can."

CHAPTER TWENTY-ONE

ALWAYS AN EAGLE

The 2017 Philadelphia Eagles will never be the same. That's the reality of professional sports. Teams change quickly. Players and coaches come and go. Free agency makes it even more difficult for winning teams to keep all their best players.

"The nature of the business is you can't keep everybody," Doug Pederson said. "It's just the way it goes. There's a side of success that's not the glamorous side. Who is going to hold out in OTAs? Who is going to want the next big contract? Who is going to miss this or that for an endorsement deal or an autograph signing? It's the not-so-glamorous side of success."

The brutal nature of the NFL meant the Eagles had to make difficult decisions based on the team's best interests from a business standpoint instead of emotional and sentimental decisions. That was evident when Brent Celek was released in March after eleven seasons in Philadelphia. The move cleared $4 million under the salary cap. Celek was a beloved leader in the locker room and a standout guy in the community. His value to the organization was reflected in a statement issued by the team after the move was announced.

"Brent Celek defines what it means to be a Philadelphia Eagle. His dedication to his profession and this organization is unmatched, and he will go down as one of the best tight ends in franchise history. Brent embodied the city of Philadelphia's temperament and character with his toughness and grit. He has been a huge part of everything we have been building over the last decade, and it is only fitting that he was able to help us win our first Super Bowl last season. Unfortunately, in this business we are forced to make difficult decisions, especially this time of the year. This one is as tough as they come, but in our eyes, Brent will always be an Eagle."

The Eagles also released Vinny Curry to save $5 million under the salary cap. Curry started every game at defensive end in the 2017 season but only had three sacks. He quickly signed a three-year, $23 million contract with the Tampa Bay Buccaneers the next day.

"It's difficult to part ways with a player like Vinny who has made an impact on the field, in the locker room, and in the community. We wish Vinny and his family all the best moving forward," the Eagles said in a statement.

Torrey Smith was traded to the Carolina Panthers, ending his short stay in Philadelphia after only one season. Smith enjoyed sharing the boldness of his Christians brothers on the team.

"It's okay to be different, it's okay to be strong in your faith," Smith said. "And for me, it wasn't really a big challenge. I have always been very comfortable in my own skin and my beliefs, but I have grown a lot over the years. I have made my mistakes, and I continue to grow each and every day. For us to have had the brotherhood that we had, it's very uplifting for all of us together."

Mychal Kendricks was released in late May in another cost-cutting move to free up $6 million under their salary cap.

Other key players the Eagles lost were free agents they couldn't afford to keep or elected not to pursue. Trey Burton signed with the Chicago Bears. LeGarrette Blount joined the Detroit Lions. Beau Allen, a defensive tackle, went to Tampa Bay. Patrick Robinson returned to the New Orleans Saints.

Success often costs teams important members on the coaching staff too. First, quarterbacks coach John DeFilippo went to the Minnesota Vikings to be their offensive coordinator on the day the Eagles held their victory parade. Then, offensive coordinator Frank Reich became the head coach of the Indianapolis Colts after Patriots offensive coordinator Josh McDaniels changed his mind following the Super Bowl and decided to stay in New England. Mike Groh was promoted from wide receivers coach to replace Reich. Press Taylor was promoted from assistant quarterbacks coach to take DeFilippo's spot.

"Those two are tremendous coaches," Nick Foles said of Reich and DeFilippo. "They were a huge reason we were so productive on offense last year and did a lot of great things. But with Coach Groh and Coach Taylor, those guys are tremendous coaches. They've been there every step of the way. I've seen Press grow every single year he's been here. They have so much knowledge, so I'm excited to work with them. They're going to do a great job."

Losing Trey Burton was a tough blow for his close friends, Carson Wentz and Zach Ertz. The trio always prayed together on the field before each game. Burton was disappointed the team didn't try to bring him back, but he got an excellent deal from the Bears worth $32 million over four years, including $22 million guaranteed.

The Eagles couldn't come close to matching that offer because Ertz is the starter.

Wentz shared an emotional goodbye to Burton on Instagram. It read, "I'm gonna miss this man, and the entire Burton family. It's crazy to think how close you can get to people in just two years. I can truly say he's one of my best friends and an amazing brother in Christ. He's a heck of a football player, but an even better follower of Christ, father, and friend. He always challenged me and encouraged me both on and off the field and I can't thank him enough for that . . . And about his family. Man oh man that's an amazing crew. I love watching the way they love on people and care for others; the way they raise their children; and the way they both pursue the Lord and make people around them better. Jax, Ariella, and Baby Kaia, you kids are amazing and I'm pretty sure I enjoyed hanging out with y'all more than I did with Trey. You guys rock and can't wait to watch you grow up! Now everybody watch this man on the Bears and know that he's about to blow up! So proud of him and happy for him! Don't worry, we'll all still hang out in the offseason . . . some place warm of course."

A few months after the Eagles won the Super Bowl, I met a college student wearing a "Philly Special" T-shirt at a speaking engagement. He told me his girlfriend was pregnant and he felt ostracized by his family and church because of it. He was questioning God and felt depressed. I encouraged him to turn to Jesus for help, guidance, and direction. I shared Burton's story and prayed with him.

A week later, I received this text: "Hey Rob. Just wanted to thank you for your encouragement and advice. I listened to your interview with Trey Burton. I can't believe Mr. Philly Special has a similar story as mine. I'm so inspired that I'm not alone. Jesus is by my side no matter what. Thank you for taking time to talk to me. It changed my life."

I shared that text with Burton and he appreciated the message.

Players are often interchangeable on the field. The Eagles signed veteran tight end Reggie Rodgers and drafted tight end Dallas Goedert in the second round to help replace Burton and Celek. The new guys may or may not be more productive. Time will tell. But Burton's leadership in the locker room and his passion to make disciples for Christ are irreplaceable. There's no doubt he'll make a major impact in Chicago.

CHAPTER TWENTY-TWO

THE NEW NORM

A new sign hanging on a wall outside the locker room at the Eagles' practice facility simultaneously celebrates the team's Super Bowl victory and sets the standard for the future. It's a picture of players holding up the Vince Lombardi Trophy with three words scrawled across the center: "The New Norm." Doug Pederson coined that term soon after the Eagles beat the Patriots. He made it known they're not satisfied with only winning one championship.

"I told them, 'If you want, get used to this. This is the new norm in Philadelphia, playing and hopefully playing into February every year. It's the new norm, so get used to it,'" Pederson said. "The guys that want to be a part of that will do that. They will want to be here. I think everybody does want to be here."

Jeffrey Lurie already was talking about ways to improve the team one day after winning the Super Bowl.

"I was obsessed to begin with," Lurie said. "I'm equally obsessed to be the first team to try to repeat in a long time. And try to put us in a position over the next several years to have an opportunity to repeat what we just accomplished."

He doesn't have to sell players on this goal. Carson Wentz is determined to deliver another Super Bowl victory to Philadelphia—this time as the starting quarterback. He told Nick Foles on the field during the celebration in Minnesota, "That's me next year." Don't bet against him. Wentz and the all-star cast of injured players who didn't get a chance to play against New England will make sure their teammates don't become complacent. Howie Roseman and his personnel staff made bold moves in the offseason—they acquired three-time Pro Bowl defensive end Michael Bennett in a trade from Seattle, signed five-time Pro Bowl defensive tackle Haloti Ngata, and wide receiver Mike Wallace in free agency—to offset losing key players. Entering training camp, the Eagles had the best odds of any NFC team to reach the 2019 Super Bowl and only the Patriots had better odds to win it. There hasn't been a repeat champion since New England did it following the 2003–2004 seasons. The Eagles are focused on breaking that trend.

"We're extremely hungry for sustained success in this city," Zach Ertz said when the team began workouts in the spring. "We've tasted it one time, and that's something that you never want to give up. We're hungry to repeat. Obviously, it's a brand-new team. You can't just do exactly what we did last year and expect to have the same result. And it's not going to be easy by any means. But we're very hungry as a football team."

Winning the Super Bowl was a life-changing experience for many of the players and coaches and fans of the Eagles. Every guy on the roster will be revered forever, especially Foles. He had a whirlwind month after the game, starting with a trip to Disney World for the Super Bowl MVP parade. He appeared on *The Ellen DeGeneres Show* and *Jimmy Kimmel Live*. He also wrote a memoir titled *Believe It: My Journey of Success, Failure and Overcoming the Odds*. But the toughest thing for Foles was getting used to seeing grown men break down in tears when they approached him in public to thank him for winning.

"I'm still the same guy. I just can't go many places," Foles said with a laugh. "It is different just walking around. It's a lot you go through. Winning the Super Bowl, being named MVP is a big stage. But I'll never change. My faith and my family are my number one priorities. That will never change."

Many of his brothers in Christ share his perspective on the ultimate victory.

"Two years ago, winning the Super Bowl would have been the best experience of my life but now with the life I am living in Christ, it was just another moment," Ertz said. "It just felt like another game. It didn't feel like the Super Bowl, a sporting event watched by a hundred million people across the world. It just felt like another game to me."

That statement may seem crazy to many people but when your identity is rooted in Christ instead of in your accomplishments, it's a standard way of thinking.

"Winning a Super Bowl doesn't fulfill," Jordan Hicks said at another *Faith On The Field Show* event at Eastern University two months after the game. "As much as you want to win and train for that and you pour so much blood, sweat, and tears into the game of football, and for that moment, it wasn't fulfilling. It's on to the next season. It's just a constant cycle of fulfillment if you put your eggs in that basket. I would say the biggest thing for me that has changed is just the platform. People want to hear the Super Bowl champion Philadelphia Eagles speak. The ability to come to events like this and across the country is a gift."

NFL players already have a wide platform they can use for influence in various ways. Winning the Super Bowl gives guys an even wider audience because more people want to listen to champions. But all Christians are called to spread the gospel no matter what they do for a living or what they've achieved. In Matthew 28:19–20, Jesus says, "Therefore go and make disciples of all nations, baptizing them in the name of the Father and of the Son and of the Holy Spirit, and teaching them to obey everything I have commanded you. And surely I am with you always, to the very end of the age."

Wentz often emphasizes this point when he has an opportunity to speak about his faith in front of a crowd.

"Making disciples, that isn't just for people who have a platform, that isn't just for people that have a million followers on Instagram or Twitter, it's for everybody," he said. "We're all called to be disciples and spread the gospel of Christ. It doesn't matter what your sphere of influence is, you have one. No matter how big or small, you're called to be a disciple in whatever mission field you're in. It's not just for pastors or people with a platform, it's for teachers, it's for businessmen. Every person you come in contact with should feel the love of Christ through you. We're all gonna have bad days. But at the end of the day, that's what we're called to do, and if you did that faithfully day after day after day, I believe on that last day, you will hear: 'Well done, good and faithful servant.'"

The 2017 Philadelphia Eagles will go down in history as Super Bowl LII champions. They'll be remembered for eternity as champions for Christ.